Humane Society Leaders in America

RICHARD MARTIN

Father of humane legislation in the British Parliament

HUMANE
SOCIETY LEADERS
IN AMERICA

With a Sketch of the Early History

of

THE HUMANE MOVEMENT IN ENGLAND

By SYDNEY H. COLEMAN

Formerly Managing Editor of

THE NATIONAL HUMANE REVIEW

PUBLISHED BY

THE AMERICAN HUMANE ASSOCIATION

ALBANY NEW YORK

1924

From the Press of
Frank H Evory & Co
Albany N Y

TABLE OF CONTENTS

ILLUSTRATIONS

THE copy for this book was written in 1922 and later revised by Dr. William O. Stillman, then President of The American Humane Association. The text was in the hands of the publisher just before Dr. Stillman's lamented death, March 15th, 1924, and appears as he arranged it.

AUTHOR

July 15, 1924

Chapter I

EARLY HISTORY OF THE HUMANE MOVEMENT

THE anticruelty movement is one hundred years old. Its history dates from that hard-won struggle in the English Parliament, waged by Richard ("Humanity") Martin, in 1822, for the first effective legislation in the world for the protection of animals. The century that has intervened since that time has been richer than all previous ages in establishing human and sub-human rights. Brilliant as has been this advancement, ages still must pass before the inequalities of life will be settled; before war ceases to be the approved mode of handling international differences; before the Golden Rule will be accepted as the true basis for man's normal guidance.

Animals were first recognized in the ethics of the Indian Aryans, probably through their acceptance of the doctrine of transmigration. Buddhism brought about a tender consideration of animals that has never been exceeded anywhere in the world. The early Persians were taught by the Zoroastrian code to treat the brute creation with kindness. Even the teachings of Islam placed the rights of animals on a par with those required by old Hebrew ethics. Seneca, Plutarch, Porphyry and other philosophers and poets, preached kindness to animals as a foundation for character building. Early Christianity reacted from these progressive views because of their pagan origin. Sub-human life was regarded as soulless and to be treated only as a vehicle by which man might achieve his selfish ends. Even the beautiful legends of animals that came from the hermit monks and the ascetics of the middle ages did little to alleviate the hard lot levied upon the brute world.

It is not difficult to understand the general disregard of animal rights, however, in view of the very general lack of sympathy for the unfortunate members of human society. Years of leavening were required before the spirit of mercy, that includes all sentient life, could make itself felt sufficiently to right the wrongs of those who could not wage their own fight for recognition. Witness in our own United States, as late as 1860, the fratricidal struggle that threatened our national life because a great section claimed the right to barter in human flesh.

Toward the close of the eighteenth century, England became greatly stirred by the writings of Jeremy Bentham, who insisted that moral rights should be the basis upon which legislation is to be founded. In the words of John Stuart Mill, " He seemed to open a clearer and broader conception of what human opinion and institutions ought to be, how they might be made what they ought to be, and how far removed from it they are now." [1] This was the period in which John Howard and Elizabeth Fry were launching their vigorous campaigns against the horrors and cruelties of the prison system. Sir Richard Oastler was leading his fight against black slavery and was soon to demand, with Sir Robert Peel, that safeguards be thrown round the health and morals of apprentices employed in cotton and other mills.

In 1800, English law recognized two hundred offenses as punishable by death. Children were hung for trivial crimes. The apprentice system had developed into child peonage that almost equalled the cruelties of black slavery. Pauper children and foundlings were virtually sold into factory drudgery where they labored from twelve to twenty hours a day, under the lash of the overseer in the midst of insanitary conditions that defy description. The mortality among these children was appalling but so engrafted was the system on the industrial life of England, that years passed before relief was secured. The prisons were stench holes and " beds of iniquity "

---

[1] Autobiography of John Stuart Mill.

into which men and women were thrown, with
little or no excuse, for debt and at the whim of
the ruling classes. The insane were incarcerated
in jails or asylums with no official inspection or
oversight. Imbecile children were disposed of by
officials for the poor by requiring that at least one
be taken with every twenty normal children ap-
prenticed to the cotton factories. What became
of them can only too readily be imagined for they
were useless to the mill owners and speedily dis-
appeared from sight.

England had long been the scene of brutal animal sports that, in a measure, compared to those
of the black days of Titus, Nero, and Trajan.
Erasmus, in describing his visit to England during the reign of Henry VIII, wrote: "Many
herds of bears are maintained in this country for
the purpose of baiting." Queen Elizabeth frequently entertained her guests with bear-baiting.
Dog, cock, and wild animal fights were the pastimes of the common people. In 1857, Thomas
Cartwright complained that "If there be a bear
or a bull to be baited in the afternoon, or a jack-
anapes to ride on horse-back, the minister hurries
the service over in shameful manner, in order to
be present at the show." [2] Sir Richard Steele
bemoaned the fact in the *Tatler,* that the French
believed the Britons had been made fierce and

---

[2] Strutt's Sports and Pastimes, 1868.

cruel by the bull-baiting, prize fighting and bear
gardens. " I wish I knew how to answer this re-
proach which is cast upon us, and excuse the
death of so many innocent cocks, bulls, dogs, and
bears, as have been set together by the ears, or
died an untimely death, only to make us sport." [3]

Gradually these sports ceased to receive royal
favor, not so much because they were degrading
as because they became scenes of rioting and dis-
cord. Bull- and bear-baiting, however, long remained the principal amusement of the lowest
and most degraded of the people. They were
not outlawed without strenuous opposition and
continued to be held clandestinely long after the
passage of the law.

The minds of men were unconsciously being
prepared for the epoch making humane legislation of 1822, by many thoughtful writers of the
eighteenth century. It is certain that only a few
of them received an extensive hearing. They did,
however, exert a powerful influence upon those
who were finally to wage an open fight in
Britain's legislative body. Bernard de Mande-
ville (1723), in his quaint and severely criticised
" Fable of the Bees," touched upon the slaughter
of animals. " I can't imagine," he wrote, " how
a man, not hardened in blood and massacre, is
able to see a violent death, and the pangs of it,

---

[3] No. 134, dated Thursday, February 16, 1709.

2

without concern." John Hildrop, M. A., published his " Free Thoughts upon the Brute Creation," in 1742. It possessed few notable features and probably had little influence in comparison with the work of the Rev. Humphrey Primatt, D.D., whose book entitled " A Dissertation on the Duty of Mercy and Sin of Cruelty to Brute Animals," was written in 1776. Some of his pleas, in behalf of the kindly care of animals were woven later into the argument of Lord Erskine during his memorable debates in Parliament for the passage of laws to protect animals from cruelty. " See that no brute of any kind," wrote Dr. Primatt, " whether intrusted to thy care, or coming in thy way, suffer thy neglect or abuse. Let no views of profit, no compliance with custom, and no fear of ridicule of the world, ever tempt thee to the least act of cruelty or injustice to any creature whatsoever. But let this be your invariable rule, everywhere, and at all times, to do unto others as, in their condition, you would be done unto."

Soame Jenyns (1704-1787), who clashed on several occasions with Samuel Johnson, devoted a chapter to the treatment of animals in his " Disquisitions on Several Subjects," published in 1772. His popularity as a politician caused his writings to be quite generally perused. Jeremy Bentham, to whom reference has been made, had a greater influence on the thought of his time than any one who had heretofore written on the humane treatment of animals. The "Introduction to the Principles of Morals and Legislation," (London, 1781), was closely studied by an increasingly large number of advanced thinkers and favorably influenced the passage of much legislation of humanitarian character. In the chapter on "Limits between Private Ethics and the Art of Legislation," Bentham shows that there is no reason why animals should not be accorded protection under the law. Then occurs this pointed sentence: "The question is not, Can they reason? nor, Can they talk? but, Can they suffer?"

The work of John Lawrence has never been given the credit it deserves in the literature of the humane movement. He was a friend of Lord Erskine and was consulted by the latter when preparing his speech on animal protection delivered in Parliament in 1809. He was a great horse fancier and frequent contributor to the *English Sporting Magazine*. Lawrence asserted that legislation was necessary before there could be universal recognition of animal rights. He pointed out the importance of teaching the child to treat his pets kindly and urged the clergy to preach on the subject of kindness to animals. He also strongly opposed the practice of vivisection. His fearless denunciation of hunting animals " of a timid and harmless na-

ture " as " a mean and contemptible exercise of
cruelty," and the riding of horses to death in the
chase as " the greatest abuse in hunting,"
brought down upon his head the wrath and ridicule of the sporting gentry. His thorough horse-
manship, however, gave him a standing in the
world of sport that caused his writings to be
eagerly read by this very class. His book, " A
Philosophical and Practical Treatise on Horses "
(London, 1796), contains many passages of such
advanced views on animal protection that they
might well have been written within the past few
years. Shortly following the publication of this
book, a bill was introduced in Parliament to prohibit bull baiting but it was so strongly opposed
that nothing came of it. Erskine was then a
member of the House of Commons. He referred
to the defeat of the measure at the time he was
making his own appeal for animal protection
legislation. Another book " On the Conduct of
Man to Inferior Animals," by George Nichol-
son, Manchester, 1797, and " An Essay on Humanity to Animals," by Thomas Young, Fellow
of Trinity College, Cambridge, London, 1798,
were other writings of this period that helped to
prepare the way for legislation for animals.

It was on May 15, 1809,[4] erroneously stated
by nearly all writers of humane history as 1811,

---

[4] Hansard, Parliamentary Debates, First Series, 14, April 11,
1809 to June 21, 1809.

that Lord Erskine arose in Parliament and delivered his carefully prepared address in behalf of the bill he had introduced for the protection of animals. This marked the first time that this subject was ever seriously debated by a powerful legislative body.[5] His speech, which was forceful and logical, subjected him to much ridicule and abuse, but he remained immovable and unperturbed. The bill passed the House of Lords and would probably have passed the Commons if it had not been introduced so late in the session. As it was, it was defeated only by a vote of 37 to 27. The following year Lord Erskine reintroduced the measure, but opposition had now grown so strong against it, in spite of many amendments to meet the wishes of his colleagues, that he withdrew it. Apparently Erskine felt the futility of following up the fight he had made so courageously in its behalf.

In Lord Erskine's opening address he had pleaded earnestly that " They (animals) are created, indeed, for our use, but not for our abuse. Their freedom and enjoyment, when they cease to be consistent with our just dominion and enjoyment, can be no part of their natures; but whilst they are consistent I say their rights, subservient as they are, ought to be as sacred as our

---

[5] When Nathaniel Ward, an English minister, who had been trained as a lawyer, prepared the first code of Massachusetts law in 1641, known as The Body of Liberties, he included a section on animal protection.

own.　*　*　*　I am to ask your Lordships, in
the name of that God who gave to man his dominion over the lower world, to acknowledge and
recognize that dominion to be a moral trust." In
closing his argument he said: " The extension of
benevolence to objects beneath us, become
habitual by a sense of duty inculcated by law,
will reflect back upon our sympathies to one another, so that I may venture to say firmly to
your Lordships, that the bill I propose to you, if it
shall receive the sanction of Parliament, will not
only be an honor to the country, but an era in the
history of the world."

The bill was opposed in a lengthy argument
by William Windham, an influential member at
that time. Among others who spoke against the
measure were Lord Ellenborough and Lord
Redesdale. The latter had been the chief opponent of the earlier bill to prohibit bull baiting.
Among those in the House of Commons who
spoke in favor of the bill were Sir Samuel
Romilly, William Wilberforce and James Stephen, all of whom were active in the anti-slavery
movement of that time.

Lord Erskine had not the satisfaction of
seeing his bill become law, but his long experience in public life must have convinced him that
it was only a matter of time before the principles
for which he contended must be recognized by
legislation. There was no justice in the charge

made against him in the debates, that the measure was introduced merely, " To have done that which no one yet had ever thought of doing; to have introduced into legislation at this period of the world, what had never been found in the laws of any country, and that, too, for the purpose of professed humanity or rather of something more than humanity as commonly understood and practiced, to be the first who had stood up as the champion of brutes, was as marked a distinction, even if it should not turn out upon examination to be as proud a one, as a man could well aspire to." [6] Many of Erskine's public acts might have justified this severe criticism by his opponent had not his love of animals always been an outstanding feature of his life. He had many pets, including " a dog that he introduced at consultations, a goose and even two leeches." [7] In 1807, he had published privately a pamphlet entitled " An Appeal in Favour of the Agricultural Services of Rooks." It must have helped to ease the unhappy close of his life to know that a new champion had arisen in Parliament for his animal friends and that his efforts to secure legislation were ultimately successful.

The new standard-bearer was Richard Martin, a member of Parliament from Galway, Ireland. Martin had been a member of the House since

---

[6] Hansard, Parliamentary Debates, First Series, 14, Page 804.
[7] Dictionary National Biography, Vol. XVII, Page 443.

1801 and probably heard Lord Erskine's masterful plea for the rights of animals in 1809. His heart must have been thrilled with the nobility of the purpose for his sense of justice and his love of animals were ruling passions of his life. On his 200,000 acre estate, there are the ruins, on the shores of Lake Ballinahinch, of an ancient structure known as " Dick Martin's Prison." In it, he was wont to confine such of his tenants as sinned against the laws of humanity towards the brute creation. He introduced bills in Parliament to abolish the death penalty for forgery, and to grant counsel for persons charged with capital crimes. His keen interest in all humanitarian measures caused George IV, his personal friend, to call him " Humanity Martin," a title by which he is fondly known to-day wherever animal protection is practiced.[8]

Martin had given the matter of animal protection no little thought and bided his time to introduce his bill in Parliament until conditions seemed propitious for prompt action. It was said by Lawrence that the law was " smuggled " through by Tory votes in spite of Liberal opposition. At any rate, Martin had to face much ridicule on the floor and overcome the objections of Lord Henry Brougham, a staunch anti-slavery reformer, and the then powerful Chan-

---

[8] Dictionary of National Biography.

ning and Peel. While Martin was speaking on his measure, a member uttered a cat-call in derision. He turned quickly in his place and said: " If the person who has just insulted me will retire to the committee room I will explain the bill to him." No one responded, for this great-hearted Irishman had a reputation as a duelist that few cared to dispute. William Jerdan relates in his chapter [9] on Martin that in one of his speeches in the House of Commons upon the subject " the orator was interrupted by ironical cheers; but he went on to the end without stop or notice and when he had finished, stepped quietly across the floor towards the quarter whence the noise had proceeded, and with infinite mildness of manner presumed to ask who it was that cried, ' Hare! Hare! ' No reply was vouchsafed to the question but one member slyly pointed to a Commoner from London as the guilty person. Martin thereupon exclaimed ' Oh! Was it only an Alderman? ' Turning on his heel he walked back to his place.

" On one occasion Martin was greatly incensed at the report of his speech in the *Morning Post*. When he called upon the editor for an explanation, the latter stated ' that it was written by one of the most intelligent and accurate reporters upon his staff, and he could hardly imagine any

[9] Men I Have Known, Pages 312-321, published by George Routledge & Sons, London, 1866.

(far less any deliberate) intention to misrepresent the Honorable gentleman.' To this excuse, the complainant only replied by pulling a copy of the paper out of his pocket and indignantly pointing to the obnoxious passage, exclaiming, ' Sir, Did I ever *spake* in Italics?' The effect was so ludicrous that both parties burst into a fit of laughter and the affair was compromised without rancor or bloodshed."

When the law was finally on the statute books, June 10, 1822 [10], it became known as " Dick Martin's Act." It marked the beginning of that " new era " that Erskine prophesied would follow the passage of such a law. Many years have elapsed since Martin's time; scores of consecrated men and women have given unstintingly of themselves to the humane cause; societies have been organized in practically every civilized country in the world for the express purpose of protecting animals from abuse, and yet the brutalizing work of the cruelist is still in evidence. The efforts put forth at such a cost, however, have not been lost. Each passing year finds the lot of additional thousands of animals made easier because of the pioneer labor of Richard Martin. He refused a peerage from his monarch, but his name has been placed among the immortals by an ever growing host of admirers throughout the world.

[10] Hansard, Volume 7, Pages 873-874.

Martin discovered, as did Bergh some forty years later in America, that the mere passage of law was not sufficient to wipe out cruelty. During the next few years that he remained in London he was constantly stopping offenders on the streets and bringing them to the bar of justice. This is particularly referred to in Burke's Vicissitudes of Families: [11] " Nor did he content himself with having obtained this parliamentary defence for his four-footed clients and then leaving the carrying of it out to others; he was equally strenuous in seeing that they had the full benefit of the law enacted for their protection." He was frequently abused by the unsympathetic public and his cases treated with derision by the courts themselves. But he never despaired. The courage that made his name respected in dueling enabled him to face his detractors fearlessly and secure justice when one less resolute must have failed.

In the *Sporting Magazine* for October, 1822, appears the report of a meeting held in September of that year at " Old Slaughter's Coffee House," in St. Martin's Lane, London, to form a society " for the preventing, as far as possible, the cruel treatment of brute animals." A committee of twelve was appointed at this time to consider ways and means. Martin was a member of this group and a leader in the movement that

[11] Fourth Edition, 1860, Page 65.

ultimately led to the organization of the Society for the Prevention of Cruelty to Animals, on June 16, 1824, at a meeting at which Rev. Arthur Broome presided. The committee drew up the following plan of operations which includes nearly every activity commonly undertaken by anticruelty societies of the present day:

" 1. The circulation of suitable tracts gratuitously, or by cheap sale, particularly among persons intrusted with cattle, such as coachmen, carters, and drovers.

" 2. The introduction into schools of books calculated to impress on youth the duty of humanity to inferior animals.

" 3. Frequent appeals to the public through the press, awakening more general attention to a subject so interesting, though too much neglected.

" 4. The periodical delivery of discourses from the pulpit.

" 5. The employment of constables in the markets and streets; and

" 6. The prosecution of persons guilty of flagrant acts of cruelty, with publicity to the proceedings, and announcements of results."

This was the first permanent organization in the world for the protection of animals. Some years before, in 1809, an advertisement appeared in the papers of Liverpool announcing a meeting for "gentlemen only" to inaugurate "The Liverpool Society for Preventing Wanton Cruelty to Brute Animals." Unfortunately, its existence was brief and feeble. Some twenty-five years later a similar effort was made by "ladies only." It also failed. The Royal Society, at London, did not begin its work of establishing branches until 1841, when those in Norwich and Liverpool were founded.

The Martin law, enacted in 1822, was known as "An Act to Prevent the Cruel and Improper Treatment of Cattle." It was the product of compromise. The popularity of hunting and other blood sports among the landed and titled classes and the demand for bull and bear baiting, and cock and dog fights among the poorer people in England made it necessary to steer a middle course in order to insure its passage. It sought to punish persons who wantonly and cruelly beat or ill-treated the horse, mare, gelding, mule, ass, ox, cow, heifer, steer, sheep or other cattle by a fine of not more than five pounds or less than ten shillings, or imprisonment not exceeding three months.

This law enabled the society to attack many of the flagrant abuses to animals that were then common, but its members were greatly disturbed because of its limitations. In 1833 an amendment was secured in Parliament which provided punishment for those who stoned or beat cattle in driving them. It was under this act that the bull, dog and lamb received their first legal protection, and the baiting and fighting of dogs, bulls, bears, badgers and cocks were prohibited. The latter provisions were so unpopular with the masses that their enforcement was delayed for several years.

Further extension of the English law was secured in 1835. At this time, any persons who " wantonly and cruelly beat, ill-treat, abuse or torture any domestic animals," became subject to the law. Those who kept or impounded animals were enjoined to feed them and those maintaining " Knackers' yards " were required to kill their animals within three days after their receipt. The early acts were amended and consolidated by the Cruelty to Animal Acts of 1849 and 1854. Under these acts the word animal was defined as any " domestic animal " of whatever kind or species, and whether a quadruped or not. The dubbing of cocks, the cropping of dogs' ears and dehorning of cattle were classified as offences. Under the act of 1854 the use of dogs for draft purposes was prohibited throughout England.

By the act of 1876 the practice of vivisection was regulated by Parliament. It was also made unlawful to maliciously poison animals. Under the " Wild Animals in Captivity Protection Act of 1900," the term " animal " is broadened to include bird, beast, fish, or reptile. Besides these acts referred to there have been many special laws passed by the British Parliament for the protection and care of animals. The acts of 1849 and 1854 are the basis upon which legislation for animals elsewhere has been founded.[12]

During the first years of the English Society, the founders struggled against great difficulties. The public was unsympathetic; funds were scant; the courts gave little assistance. Yet the Society kept tenaciously at its task, educating people to higher regard for the rights of the brute world and warning and prosecuting those guilty of cruelty.

Royalty eventually took note of its good work. Queen Victoria became its patron and in 1840 gave permission to attach the prefix Royal to its title. Since that time its work has grown to large proportions. Its agents are scattered throughout England, Wales and Ireland. A vast amount of valuable humane literature has been prepared and published. Its chief publication is the *Animal World* which was suggested to its Secretary, John Colam, in 1869, by George T. Angell, of Boston. The magazine has been published continuously since that date and is regarded as one of the finest of its class.

---

[12] The Law Relating to the Prevention of Cruelty to Animals, London, 1906. For a rather full account of humane legislation for animals, see an article by George A. H. Scott, published in *The National Humane Review*, Vol. IV, Pages 3, 4, 23, 46, 47, 57, and 70.

The active direction of the Royal Society for the Prevention of Cruelty to Animals is at present in the hands of its able Chief Secretary, Captain Edward G. Fairholme, who is well known to American humanitarians. He visited this country in 1910 to take part in the International Humane Congress held in Washington, and again in 1923 to attend the Second American World Humane Conference. The Royal Society provided many thousands of dollars worth of veterinary supplies and built several hospitals for the horses of the British forces during the world war of 1914-1918. The Royal S. P. C. A. also furnished a considerable personnel toward staffing the hospitals, and many assistants to the veterinary corps. Secretary Fairholme was honored with the commission of a Captain for his valuable services in this direction. He also materially aided the American Red Star Animal Relief in having motor veterinary ambulances manufactured for it in England, which were presented to the American forces in France.

HENRY BERGH
*Founder and President of the American Society for
the Prevention of Cruelty to Animals, 1866 to 1888*

Chapter II

HENRY BERGH: FOUNDER OF THE ANTICRUELTY CAUSE IN AMERICA

IT was more than a mere coincidence that the humane movement in England and America followed so closely upon the abolition of human slavery. The Parliamentary Acts of 1807 and 1811 stamped out slavery within the British Empire. These laws were the outgrowth of years of the most intense agitation in behalf of the principles of human liberty for all people, regardless of race or color. It was in 1809 that Erskine made his famous plea that animals were entitled to legal protection. How Martin's Act, in 1822, became the first legislative recognition of this principle has been related in the previous chapter.

Lincoln's Emancipation Proclamation was issued in 1863, and was followed in 1865 by a constitutional amendment that abolished and forever prohibited slavery within the United States. But the curse of involuntary servitude was only wiped out through the blood and tears of a great Civil War. By it the rights of the defenseless were established. The conscience of a nation was stirred to its depths, and resulted in the development of an era of humanitarian progress heretofore unknown. Under such conditions it was most natural that the unfortunate lot of animals should attract attention. Ten years earlier such a movement could not have flourished. But in 1866, the stage was set and it only needed the inspiration of a stalwart leader to insure its success.

Henry Bergh was such a character. He believed himself divinely called to this work. None was more fitted by birth, education or temperament to inaugurate and carry on a difficult and unpopular crusade. He was the son of Christian Bergh, a wealthy and highly respected shipbuilder of New York City. In the Bergh yards were built some of the finest ships used in the War of 1812. Christian Bergh was a man of sterling worth and resolute will, qualities that were transmitted to his son Henry in no small degree. His ancestors came from Germany during the early part of the eighteenth century and settled along the lower Hudson. Christian married Elizabeth Ivers, the daughter of a substantial Connecticut family, who exerted a splendid influence over her children. Henry Bergh was born in New York City, May 8th, 1823, and died there March 12th, 1888. He had one brother and a sister.

On the death of the shipmaster, the large estate was divided among the three children. Henry soon disposed of his interest in the ship-yard, preferring to devote his life to literature and play writing. His early education was thorough and completed by a course at Columbia University. He did not remain to graduate, leaving college for extensive travel in Europe. He returned to the United States in 1848 and soon after married Matilda Taylor, daughter of a wealthy Englishman, residing in New York. The next twelve years were spent in Europe and the Far East. During the latter portion of this period he resided in Germany, where he did considerable writing. His wide travels and familiarity with life on the Continent caused President Lincoln to appoint him Secretary of Legation and Acting Consul at St. Petersburg, in 1862.

During Bergh's trips over Europe he had been repeatedly shocked by the ill-treatment accorded animals, for which he had manifested a great liking since early boyhood. While in St. Petersburg, he discovered that with the aid of his liveried footman he could successfully intervene in many cases of cruelty which he witnessed because of the respect shown by the common people to official uniforms. One day after his servant had induced a man to cease beating his donkey, Bergh said: " At last I've found a way to utilize my gold lace and about the best use I can make of it."

Owing to ill-health, Mr. Bergh was obliged to resign his post in 1864, but not before he had established most friendly relations at the royal court. As a special mark of favor the emperor's private yacht was, on one occasion, placed at his disposal to visit the naval station of Kronstadt. Secretary Seward wrote that the Government accepted Mr. Bergh's resignation with great reluctance.

The daily scenes of cruelty to animals on the streets of St. Petersburg so moved Mr. Bergh that he resolved to return to America and devote the remainder of his life to the cause of animal protection. On his way home he visited London and studied the work of the Royal Society for the Prevention of Cruelty to Animals, which at that time had forty years of glorious achievement to its credit. Mr. Bergh reached New York in the fall of 1864 and began immediately to shape the plans for his future work. He realized fully the difficulties that confronted him; the indifference of the people to suffering; the ridicule of unfriendly newspapers; the hatred of those whose pleasure or profits would be curtailed through his interference; the cost in money and physical strength; and, not least, the loss of personal friendships among those who would not understand that his motives were unselfish and prompted only by a sincere desire to stop suffering wherever he found it.

At the outset his efforts met with little encouragement. The public was experiencing the reactions following four trying years of war. But Bergh would not give up, though he was greatly disheartened. He continued to interview prominent persons and enlist their support. Some of the leading newspapers were induced to feature his plans, which brought them to the attention of thousands throughout the city. His preliminary work must have been well done for, in spite of slush and rain, a good sized audience of representative citizens, including ex-Governor, then Mayor, John T. Hoffman, A. T. Stewart and other well-known men and women, braved the weather to hear him lecture on the cause of animal protection, in Clinton Hall, on the evening of February 8, 1866. His appeal was direct and convincing. "This is a matter purely of conscience," he said. "It has no perplexing side issues. Politics have no more to do with it than astronomy, or the use of the globe. No, it is a moral question in all its aspects; it addresses itself to that quality of our nature that can not be disregarded by any people with safety to their dearest interests; it is a solemn recognition of that greatest attribute of the Almighty Ruler of the Universe, mercy, which if suspended in our own case but for a single instant, would overwhelm and destroy us."

At the close of his lecture, several gentlemen
assured him of their willingness to aid him financially and morally. The press in New York and
in nearly all of the large cities, featured his remarks. Their novel character attracted a wide
reading and led many to proffer their assistance.
Mr. Bergh was more encouraged than he had
been in many a day. He realized, however, that
permanent results could only be secured through
the medium of an incorporated society, invested
with power to bring the cruelist to justice. He
accordingly went to Albany with the necessary
papers and asked the legislature for a state-wide
charter for the American Society for the Prevention of Cruelty to Animals. This was granted on
April 10, 1866, in spite of vigorous opposition by
some of the legislators. It was the first document
of its kind in the Western Hemisphere—the fore-
runner and the pattern of many to be issued
within a brief period. The document was drawn
by James T. Brady and bore the signatures of
ex-Governor Hoffman, J. J. Astor, Jr., John A.
Dix, Peter Cooper, C. V. S. Roosevelt, George
Bancroft and many other prominent New York-
ers.

The only law on the New York statute books
dealing with animal protection was one that had
been passed in 1829. It was inadequate and had
long been a dead letter. Mr. Bergh submitted a
bill to the legislature which was passed April

19, 1866, the anniversary of the Battle of Lexington. It was to be equally as significant in the cause of animal protection as was that famous skirmish of American patriots in their struggle for human liberty. Opposition developed to this " innovation," but Bergh declared that had he thought the bill would pass so easily he would have asked for more. As it was the law now provided that " every person who shall, by his act or neglect, maliciously kill, maim, wound, injure, torture, or cruelly beat any horse, mule, cow, cattle, sheep, or other animal, belonging to himself or another, shall, upon conviction, be adjudged guilty of a misdemeanor." The law was avowedly tentative in character. Mr. Bergh anticipated, as events later proved to be the case, that as experience grew in the application of the act, it would be possible to work out more carefully planned legislation.

Three days after the passage of the law, April 22, 1866, a meeting was called in Clinton Hall, at which the mayor presided. At that time the American Society for the Prevention of Cruelty to Animals was formally organized. Its purpose as set forth in its constitution was: " To provide effective means for the prevention of cruelty to animals throughout the United States, to enforce all laws which are now or may hereafter be enacted for the protection of animals and to secure, by lawful means, the arrest and conviction of all persons violating such laws."

Henry Bergh was unanimously elected as the society's first president, a position he continued to hold until his death in 1888. George Bancroft, the celebrated historian, was made a vice-president, and many other well-known persons were placed on the Board of Directors. At the close of Mr. Bergh's brief address of acceptance, he said: " This, gentlemen, is the verdict that you have this day rendered, that the blood-red hand of cruelty shall no longer torture dumb animals with impunity."

" That same evening," writes a contemporary, " Henry Bergh buttoned his overcoat and went forth to defend the law he had been mainly instrumental in securing, aware that on himself more than on any other man depended whether they were laughed at or obeyed." He had not long to wait before he found a driver beating his horse. " My friend, you can't do that any more," politely interceded Mr. Bergh. " The d—— I can't," was the laconic reply, and the whip was laid on with renewed vigor. Mr. Bergh protested, but was told to mind his own business.

" I saw it was necessary to make an impression in order to bring the law before the public," said Mr. Bergh. Afterwards, in speaking of the affair, Mr. Bergh said that it was because of this conviction that he often adopted spectacular methods in handling cases of cruelty. Few reformers have more fully realized the value of newspaper publicity, even though at times it made him the butt of cheap wits and the target for cartoons. His long, angular face lent itself readily to pencil and pen sketches, a feature that cartoonists were not slow to grasp. He probably bore in mind the advice once given him by a Cheapside publisher in London, to whom he complained that the critics had been unfair in their reviews of his poem " Married Off." " If you are bound to appear in print," consoled the publisher, " well and good if the newspapers speak in praises of you; but next to praise, being cut to pieces is the best thing to be hoped for. What we have to fear is that we will not be noticed at all. Silence is fatal."

Two attic rooms, at Broadway and Fourth Street, New York, were promptly rented by the society for office purposes. Mr. Bergh patrolled the streets, acted as agent, prosecutor and chief executive. Frequently he was obliged to pay its bills. But he persevered. He recognized the justice of his mission and nothing could induce him to turn back. Every item of expense was carefully considered and every cent received was placed where it would do the most good for the animals for which he labored. Once when Governor Hoffman visited the office he stumbled over a hole in the ragged carpet on the floor.

" Why, Mr. Bergh," he remarked, " do you not have a better carpet? Buy one and send the bill to me." " No, Governor," replied Mr. Bergh, " that will never do; the animals need it; send the money to me and I will put it to better use on the streets."

Among the first abuses to receive the attention of the new society was the barbarous methods of transporting live calves in carts. These little creatures were tied by the legs and often piled on top of each other in such a way as to endanger their eyes and subject them to great physical suffering. Mr. Bergh resolved to break up the practice and caused the arrest of a Brooklyn butcher, who was convicted of the offense on April 25, 1866, and fined $10.00. A similar case the following day resulted in conviction, a fine of $10.00 and further sentence of one day in the penitentiary. These were the first recorded convictions for cruelty to animals in America. Another early campaign was directed against the plucking of live fowl. The press devoted much attention to the campaign, with very beneficial results.

But the general public was still apathetic and Mr. Bergh longed for some case that would turn the spotlight on the society and give it space on the front page of the newspapers. The discovery of a boatload of live turtles that had been shipped from Florida on their backs, with their flippers

pierced and tied together with strings, offered
this opportunity. When the captain of the ves-
sel refused to turn the turtles over, Mr. Bergh
caused his arrest, together with the members of
his crew. They were taken to the Tombs, but
were later acquitted of cruelty by the court, although the famous Agassiz came to Mr. Bergh's
rescue with a brief stating " that the Great Crea-
tor, in endowing it (turtle) with life, gave to it
feeling and certain rights, as well as to our-
selves." The judge, before whom the case was
tried, told Bergh to go home and mind his own
business. Some of the newspapers charged him
with being overzealous and many abused him
roundly. A lengthy satire in the *New York
Herald,* a few days later, set all New York talking. For a time James Gordon Bennett continued to systematically ridicule Bergh and his
society, but later the two men became personal
friends and the *Herald* one of the staunchest supporters of the movement. The final outcome of
the turtle case was to greatly increase the number of supporters and friends of the new society.

The society created quite a stir by exposing
stock food dealers who were adulterating horse
and cattle food with marble dust. Mr. Bergh
also found time to appeal for better street pavements and to break up dog fights, which were then
very popular with the scum of society and a certain class of wealthy " sports."

The cruelty of overloading and using unfit animals on omnibuses and street railways was so glaring an evil that Mr. Bergh opened a fight against it during the first year of the society. He prosecuted it with great vigor for several years until drivers and owners came to understand that such practices would not be permitted. Nothing did more for the advancement of the society than this campaign. Mr. Bergh would station himself at the junction of two or more lines and examine the team and load of every car that passed. If the load was too heavy he would compel some of the passengers to alight, or if one or both of the horses were unfit for service he suspended them from work. On one occasion he held up an overloaded street car during a severe snow storm. The ill-fed, overworked team was struggling to start the car with its mass of human freight which overflowed onto the platform and even struggled to retain a footing on the lower step, when Mr. Bergh loomed out of the storm. When the driver demanded by what authority he interfered, Bergh displayed his badge and ordered a number of the passengers to get off. The act was not a popular one with the passengers, who had paid their fare and were being inconvenienced, but their remonstrances were lost on Bergh, who stood at the horses' heads and refused to permit the car to proceed. Finally a big, burly rough came forward and, hurling an unmentionable epithet, shook his fist under Mr. Bergh's nose. Without a moment's hesitation he grabbed the fellow and with a mighty heave threw him into a snowbank. The crowd, which a second before had been hostile, gave a hearty cheer for the hero of the moment and without another protest got off the car and walked home.[1]

The victory against the overloading of horse cars was not won without a legal battle. When Mr. Bergh was informed that he would not be able to secure legislation regulating the carrying capacity of the cars he decided to make a test case in the courts under the existing law. Accordingly a driver and a conductor were arrested and tried before a jury. Both were convicted and fined $250.00. This verdict was appealed but sustained by the Supreme Court. This and similar cases were contested bitterly by the street railway company through the most eminent counsel. The decision was a great victory for the society and Mr. Bergh.

Before the end of the society's first fiscal year, he had been to Albany and secured a law from the legislature limiting the time cattle could be left on the cars without food or water, in New York State, to twenty-eight hours. This was the first legislation to regulate the shipment of live stock. At a later date he was able, with the help

---

[1] Henry Bergh's First Victory, Clara Morris, McClure's Magazine, March, 1902.

of Elbridge T. Gerry, to reduce this time limit to twenty-four hours. He also started a movement for the erection of drinking fountains for animals that has since been energetically extended to many other cities.

At the second annual meeting of the American Society for the Prevention of Cruelty to Animals, held in the spring of 1867, Mr. Bergh said: " Before the formation of the corporation, so little attention had been given by the people of this country to the prevention of cruelty to animals, that many of the best informed persons, and those of the most benevolent characteristics generally, appeared to be unconscious of the gross ignorance, thoughtlessness, indifference, and wanton cruelty to which the brute creation was daily subjected." While a year's work had not entirely altered this condition, it had done much to correct it. Some of the original supporters had become disheartened by the ridicule and abuse heaped upon them, but others had felt prompted to fill in the gaps and the membership and financial support were constantly increasing. Frank Leslie had placed his influential publication right back of Mr. Bergh and did yeoman service in winning moral support for the society. Sixty-six convictions were secured out of 119 prosecutions during these first eventful twelve months, a record that many societies of a later day, under far more auspicious circumstances,

have not equalled. More than \$7,400 was re-
ceived for the support of the society, in the first
year of its existence.

The second year began with Mr. Bergh more
convinced than ever that his task was a holy one
and deserved his unremitting efforts. The importance of reaching the children with humane
instruction was realized by him and led him to
speak before many audiences of school children.
He also reached the rural districts for the first
time in the history of the humane movement by
delivering an address at the Putnam County
Fair. The speech was widely quoted in farm
publications.

One of the most sensational of the campaigns
waged by Mr. Bergh was directed against the use
of " swill milk." After vainly attempting to interest the health department in the sanitary aspects of the case, he disclosed the frightfully insanitary conditions under which much of the
city's milk supply was produced. Cattle in the
last stages of disease, frequently so weak that
they could only be kept on their feet with slings,
were housed and milked in underground stables
that reeked with filth and foul odors. They were
fed on distillery slops and garbage. The start-
ling revelations created a sensation which the
papers featured prominently. Prosecutions instituted by Mr. Bergh against those guilty of
such improper and disgusting practices met with

the most unexpected obstacles.   Cases were adjourned and postponed.   Several defendants were acquitted.   One justice refused to permit Mr. Bergh to appear in the case, in spite of the fact that he enjoyed a permanent appointment as " assistant district attorney."   Even the evidence of experts was denied by the politically corrupt court before which the cases were tried. Finally, Frank Leslie, James Gordon Bennett and other powerful editors joined him in the fight which ultimately resulted in the state authorities taking a hand and abating the evils.

New York City was infested with scores of places in the lowest parts of the city where dog and cock fights, rat-baiting and other equally bloody and degrading sports were held with little or no interference from the police.   Mr. Bergh opened a vigorous fight upon these cruelties, often exposing himself to great physical danger in the raids that he led against them.   So greatly did they fear him that his house and the offices of the society were picketed in an attempt to frustrate his raids.   He and his agents were shadowed for months.   The courts were not always willing to punish these offenders, and all manner of influence was brought to divert Mr. Bergh from his purpose.   After he had successfully raided and brought to justice the notorious Kit Burns, the acknowledged leader of the dog fighting fraternity, the pastime was pursued with greater

Headquarters of the American Society for Prevention of Cruelty to Animals, 50 Madison Avenue, New York

caution than before. At the trial, Burns said to Mr. Bergh: " Your society is doing a noble work, sir, yes, a magnificent work, but let me tell you, when it interferes in dog fighting, it digs its own grave."

Mr. Bergh was fast achieving a country wide reputation. He was deluged with inquiries which came to him from all parts of America for advice and suggestions regarding animal protection work. These communications received his personal attention and the replies that he wrote out with painstaking care were often the stimulus which led to the formation of local anticruelty societies. On invitation of societies that had already been incorporated in Boston and Philadelphia, he visited those places in 1869 and delivered inspirational addresses before large audiences. Requests for lectures were numerous, but he seldom felt that he could leave his work in New York for that purpose. In 1873, he finally acceded to urgent invitations and planned a lecture tour that included Buffalo, Cleveland, Toledo, Chicago, St. Louis, Louisville and Cincinnati. Everywhere he was greeted by distinguished audiences. In Buffalo, where a Branch of his own society was organized in 1868, Hon. Millard Fillmore presided at the meeting. In other instances the governor of the state, or the mayor of the city in which he spoke, honored him by acting as the chairman of his meeting. He

4

had become a national figure.   The story of his
crusade against cruelty had aroused a vast number of people to action.   Those who crowded the
lecture halls to hear him, listened with rapt attention to his message, which was marked with
pathos and humor.   There was something in the
tone of his voice, the flash of the deep-set eyes, the
sway of the tall, gaunt form, that fired the enthusiasm of those who heard him to go forth and
emulate his good works.

Many notable improvements in the handling
of sick and disabled animals were being worked
out under his personal supervision.   In 1869, he
devised the horse ambulance which greatly facili-
tated the moving of sick or injured animals unable to walk.   So well did he work out the design
that with the exception of substituting motor for
horse power, little change has been made in the
construction of horse ambulances since that time.
It is an interesting fact that ambulance service
for animals was introduced before it was adopted
by hospitals for humans. Mr. Bergh also adapted
the derrick for lifting horses out of excavations.
He early took a decided stand against vivisection
and never lost an opportunity to oppose it.

Live pigeon shoots were very popular with gun
clubs during the early seventies.   They were attended with so much suffering to wounded birds
that Mr. Bergh attacked the sport in his usual
vigorous way, thereby bringing down upon him

the enmity of sporting clubs. His relentless fight
caused the invention of the clay pigeon, to which
he gave the greatest encouragement. In a test
case it was held that the shooting of live pigeons
thrown from traps came under the general cruelty act. This aroused the ire of the pigeon
shooters and the manufacturers of sporting
goods, who succeeded in inducing the legislature
to pass a law legalizing the sport. Every move
was bitterly opposed by Mr. Bergh, Mr. Gerry
and other humanitarians, but without avail.
Numerous attempts were made to repeal the law,
including one by Theodore Roosevelt, but the
law remained on the statute books until 1901.

By 1870, the work had grown to such proportions that Mr. Bergh could not look after the
corps of agents on the streets, attend to the increasing office work and give the legal details the
attention which they deserved. Previously he
had personally prosecuted nearly all of the
society's cases. Those who opposed him before
the bar recognized him as no mean lawyer. He
cross-examined with ingenious skill and often
succeeded in placing the defense in an awkward
position. When the courts failed to render what
he regarded to be plain justice to his animal clients he did not hesitate to assail their decisions.
At one time the situation became so bad that it
was with difficulty that he got his cases before
the courts, but his intrepid courage drove him on

until at last he won the recognition which he
knew to be his due.

Fortunately he was able to enlist the volunteer
services of Elbridge T. Gerry, a brilliant young
attorney, who was to win undying fame later in
his work for child protection.   Mr. Gerry, with
his well trained legal mind, threw his whole energy into helping Mr. Bergh prosecute his work.
His skill on one occasion saved Mr. Bergh from
conviction on the ground of making a " false arrest," and on another he caused a presentment by
the Grand Jury to be quashed.   In the latter instance Mr. Bergh had criticised the jury for its
failure to hear witnesses he had produced against
some cock fighters.   After Mr. Gerry's connection with the society, he prepared all legislation
offered by it in Congress or the state legislature,
and made many arguments before legislative
committees in its behalf.   His aid was invaluable
in Bergh's legislative fight to prevent the street
car company from using salt to thaw out its
switches, the salt causing injuries to the horses'
feet.   The persistency with which the society
caused its bill to be reintroduced, year after year,
ultimately resulted in the desired legislation.

The unyielding tactics of Mr. Bergh in his
legislative campaigns are well illustrated by the
following, quoted from the society's report for
1873:   " ' Why,' remarked a senator, while our
bill was under consideration in that branch of the

legislature, ' why these humanitarians will by and
by tell us that we should be tender in the treatment of the rat, the reptile, and the bug.' ' Yes,
Mr. Senator, you are right; only your prediction
is not comprehensive enough, for the by and by
is now present, ever has been, and ever will be,
because it is an attribute of the Deity and of His
World. Kill, if necessary, but torture not, is the
command of intelligent reason.' "

From the earliest days of Mr. Bergh's activities he had realized the need of legislation to
regulate the transportation of animals on the
railroads. Frequently food animals were kept
on stock trains for eighty hours or more without
food or water. Shipments of live stock were left
for hours on side tracks that perishable fruit and
dead freight might be rushed to their destination.
During 1867, as we have stated, he induced the
New York legislature to place a twenty-eight
hour time limit on shipments of live stock within
the state. At a later date the time limit was reduced to twenty-four hours. If the shipment
were consigned to some point outside the state,
there was no law to prevent the animals from
being kept on board till they starved to death, a
condition that actually occurred at times through
the indifference of railroad employees. Mr.
Gerry caused a bill to be introduced in Congress
to regulate such shipments. After a hard fight,
participated in by many humanitarians, the so-

called twenty-eight hour law was passed. This was ultimately amended to allow live stock to be confined in cars for thirty-six hours, without feed or water, under certain special conditions which, however, are deemed unsatisfactory.

Early in the life of the society Mr. Bergh found himself hampered by lack of sufficient funds with which to prosecute his work. During the first year Mr. and Mrs. Bergh turned over to the society a property that would yield about $7,000 annually. Some legacies were promised. Money came from persons of whom Mr. Bergh had never heard, but who had been impressed with the importance of his work through the accounts in the press. One of the most notable of these legacies was that of a benevolent Frenchman, by the name of Louis Bonard, who sent for Mr. Bergh just before he died at St. Vincent's hospital. " I have," said the sick man, " long entertained a deep regard for the Society for the Prevention of Cruelty to Animals, and I have bequeathed it all my property, as there is no other cause which so entirely possesses my sympathies as the one it represents." His estate amounted to more than $150,000, but the will was so vigorously contested by relatives that the society realized only about $100,000. The property was not finally conveyed to the society until 1873 and was then used to purchase permanent headquarters at Fourth Avenue and 22nd Street.

The Animal Kingdom, the second humane publication in America, was founded by Mr. Bergh in 1873, and continued to be published until 1907. It served as a splendid vehicle for keeping the members and friends of the society informed of its progress in the field of animal protection.

One of the most notable achievements of Henry Bergh was the founding of the Society for the Prevention of Cruelty to Children in 1874, in conjunction with Mr. Elbridge T. Gerry. It was the first organized attempt in the world to rescue neglected and abused children and marked the beginning of a movement that was to revolutionize the lot of unfortunate childhood. Its development is described in another chapter of this book.

During the last few years of Mr. Bergh's life he suffered from indigestion, but did not cease to exert himself in behalf of the society for which he had sacrificed so much, up to the time of his death on March 12th, 1888. During the twenty-three years the society had been in existence, he had been in supreme command of its affairs, though he had depended to no small extent upon the counsel of his friend, Elbridge T. Gerry. When he died, *The New York Herald* said: "His society was distinctly a one man power. The Society for the Prevention of Cruelty to Animals was Henry Bergh and Henry Bergh was the Society for the Prevention of Cruelty to Animals." He once said: " I hate to think what will become of this society when I am gone." Fortunately, there were those who were willing to carry on the work. At the time of this writing the American Society for the Prevention of Cruelty to Animals continues to be one of the largest organizations of its kind in the world, both in the extent of work performed and in financial resources. What a monument it is to him whose creative genius founded and developed the work in spite of great obstacles and opposition.

Many of the papers that had in the early days held Mr. Bergh up to ridicule, devoted extensive space to his obituary, praising his life work and according him the recognition that he so rightfully deserved. The friends of animals everywhere mourned his passing. For so many years he had stood as the most prominent figure in humanitarian enterprise, that to some it seemed as though the keystone of the arch had been removed. His staunch friend and co-laborer, Elbridge T. Gerry, was moved to write in the resolutions on his death prepared for the American Society for the Prevention of Cruelty to Animals: " And now that he has passed away in the fulness of years, his memory unimpaired, his intellect clear to the last, and his name untarnished and lustrous through the course of a long and

Mr. William K. Horton
*General Manager, the American Society for the
Prevention of Cruelty to Animals since 1906*

busy life consecrated to the noblest work of charity—the care of the helpless—where shall his
equal be found who will leave so great a name?
When will his like appear again? "

A sketch of Henry Bergh would be incomplete that failed to give a picture of his unique
personality. If his education and extensive
travel gave him an urbanity that commanded the
attention of the most illustrious people of his
day; if his wealth enabled him to devote himself
unreservedly to his task for twenty-three years
without remuneration of any kind, other than the
satisfaction of doing good; his physical appearance, his ability to withstand unjust criticism and
scurrilous attacks of bitter enemies, were equally
responsible for his success. We will let those
who saw him as he went about the streets of New
York, alert for acts of cruelty, describe him:

" I was alarmed by the dignity of his presence
and disarmed by his politeness. Since Horace
Greeley's death, no figure more familiar to the
public has walked the streets of the metropolis.
Nature gave him an absolute patent on every
feature and manner of his personality. His commanding stature of six feet is magnified by his
erect and dignified bearing. A silk hat with
straight rim covers with primness the severity of
his presence. A dark brown or dark blue frock
overcoat encases his broad shoulders and spare,
yet sinewy, figure. A decisive hand grasps a

cane, strong enough to lean upon, and competent to be of defense without looking like a standing menace. When this cane, or even his finger, is raised in warning, the cruel driver is quick to understand and heed the gesture. On the crowded street, he walks with a slow, slightly swinging pace peculiar to himself. Apparently preoccupied, he is yet observant of everything about him and mechanically notes the condition of every passing horse. Everybody looks into the long, solemn, finely chiseled face wearing an expression of firmness and benevolence. Brown locks fringe a broad and rounded forehead. Eyes between blue and hazel, lighted by intellectual fires, are equally ready to dart authority or show compassion. There is energy of character in a long nose of the purest Greek type; melancholy in a mouth rendered doubly grave by deep lines, thin lips and a sparse, drooping mustache, and determination in a square chin of leonine strength. The head, evenly poised, is set on a stout neck rooted to broad shoulders. In plainness, gravity, good taste, individuality and unassuming and self-possessed dignity, his personality is a compromise between a Quaker and a French nobleman whose life and thoughts no less than long descent are his title to nobility."

Drivers knew him and touched their caps to him, a courtesy he always acknowledged with a friendly smile and a nod of his head. Often strangers would grasp his hand and assure him of their cooperation and friendship. He was a ready speaker and never at a loss for a reply. On one occasion when Police Justice " Joe " Dowling (as he was commonly known) rendered a decision according to his own view of what the law ought to be, with the remark, " That is Joe Dowling's law," Mr. Bergh retorted. " Some day there will be a Bergh law which you will obey or we shall try to compel you to do so."

Frequently he would take advantage of a crowd that gathered around when he stopped a driver for some offense to deliver a little lesson on Americanism and kindness. It became known as his curbstone address: " Now, gentlemen, consider that you are American citizens, living in a republic. You make your own laws: no despot makes them for you. And I appeal to your sense of justice and your patriotism, ought not you to respect what you yourselves have made? "

Mr. Bergh's physical strength is a matter often referred to among the anecdotes preserved of his work. When moral suasion failed to secure desired results, he did not hesitate to use brute force. One day he found a cart loaded with calves and sheep. The legs of the poor creatures were bound and their heads hung over the sides of the vehicle. When the driver and helper refused to relieve them of their suffering, Mr.

Bergh pulled the two men off the cart and holding them at arm's length brought their heads together with a thud. " How do you like that exercise? " he inquired. " Perhaps now you can feel how the heads of those poor sheep and calves feel."

Among all classes of people Bergh commanded attention and respect but he never had or sought many close personal friends. His position in society and his reserve kept his inferiors from taking liberties with him. One acquaintance for whom he showed marked regard was a young prize fighter who studied law and later became a successful criminal lawyer. Bergh enjoyed his society and on one occasion took dinner at his West Side home. Mr. Bergh declared afterwards, " He is one of nature's noblemen, cares for his mother and loves all animals."

It was commonly thought that he was callous to ridicule but few were more sensitive to the criticism of friends and enemies. His wife, who was his loyal supporter and gave him moral encouragement when things looked black, said that he often cried over the vexatious difficulties that were heaped in his way. In spite of this sensitiveness, he did not let it interfere with his crusade. He once said: " Two or three years of ridicule and abuse have thickened the epidermis of my sensibilities, and I have acquired the habit of doing the thing I think right, regardless of public clamor."

If animal protection was Mr. Bergh's hobby, the theatre was his delight. He was an inveterate "first nighter" and possessed a wonderful knowledge of the spoken drama. It was his ambition as a young man to become a playwright. He produced several comedies that were tried out unsuccessfully in England. Only one of his plays, "Hard Sex," was produced in America, and that privately. He also wrote several poems. Henry Bergh's literary efforts have long been forgotten, but his name will always be associated with the inauguration of a great reform. Every state in the Union has testified to the soundness of his work by passing legislation for animal protection modeled after the laws which he caused to be enacted in New York State. He saw the child of his thoughts grow from an idea to a mighty and successful institution. He witnessed more than 12,000 cases of cruelty prosecuted by his society. He beheld scores of societies for the protection of animals started all over the Union. He inaugurated a movement that has rescued several million children from neglect and crime. His work vitalized the Golden Rule and gave it added sway in the hearts of his countrymen. Surely such achievements entitle Henry Bergh to place among the noblest of America's immor-

tals. The poet Longfellow paid a justly deserved tribute to Mr. Bergh when he wrote:

" Among the noblest of the land,
    Though he may count himself the least,
    That man I honor and revere,
    Who, without favor, without fear,
    In the great city dares to stand
    The friend of every friendless beast."

Soon after the death of Henry Bergh the
American Society for the Prevention of Cruelty
to Animals elected his nephew and namesake,
Henry Bergh, as his successor. This gentleman
had long been associated and in the fullest sympathy with the work of his distinguished uncle.
He still continues to be closely identified with
the society. In 1890, John P. Haines was elected
President and remained in office for sixteen years.
During this time the society took over the dog
license and municipal pound work which previously had been in charge of the city. The
change proved very satisfactory. The society
further modernized its work by installing motor
ambulances for large and small animals, which
was something new in the humane world and
marked a great step in advance. This period
was further marked by the erection of an attractive and convenient headquarters building in the
heart of New York, at the corner of Madison
Avenue and Twenty-sixth Street, opposite Madison Square Garden.

In 1907, Col. Alfred Wagstaff was elected President. He had been previously a co-worker with the elder Bergh and was deeply interested in the operations of the society. His administration proved a very successful one and he served until his death in October, 1921. His successor was Mr. Frank K. Sturgis, a gentleman of signal ability, who was elected soon after Col. Wagstaff's decease. His selection proved a happy choice and he has served the society to the satisfaction of its many friends. He still occupies the position of President.

Much of the successful administration of the American Society for the Prevention of Cruelty to Animals, during the past quarter of a century, and more, has been due to the devoted services of William K. Horton as General Manager. He has been in the employ of the society since 1895, and brought to his office services of the highest order. To him, in cooperation with President Wagstaff, largely belongs the credit for the erection of the first modern Animal Hospital, to increase the usefulness of an anticruelty society. This building, which is a model of efficiency, cleanliness and equipment, is the result of many years of careful planning and a very liberal expenditure of money. The society waited until it could appropriate some $200,000 for an institution which would meet modern requirements. Mr. Horton has helped to modernize the ambulance department, to equip watering stations for horses and to develop an effective system of humane education in the public schools of New York. He has done much to encourage more humane slaughtering of food animals and has been a wise and enlightened administrator for a great and progressive anti-cruelty society, the success of which has been very largely dependent on his devotion for many years.

During all these years Henry Bergh's society has gone steadily forward in its work for humanity. It operates more than a score of automobiles and has more than one hundred persons on its payroll. The society has steadily gained in public esteem and support. It is safe to say that it has deserved it.

Hon. Elbridge T. Gerry

*President, New York Society for the Prevention of
Cruelty to Children, 1876 to 1901*

CHAPTER III

ELBRIDGE T. GERRY AND THE PREVENTION OF CRUELTY TO CHILDREN

CHILD saving work in America was so long and so closely associated with the name of Elbridge T. Gerry that the New York Society for the Prevention of Cruelty to Children became generally known as " the Gerry Society." This was a public tribute to his untiring energy, faithful devotion and legal sagacity, so freely given to protect the interests of the society and its pitiful clients. For years Mr. Gerry was generally acknowledged as the foremost champion of oppressed childhood in the United States.

The New York Society for the Prevention of Cruelty to Children was the first of its kind in the world. Its efficiency was largely due to Mr. Gerry, who formulated the laws under which it operated and steadfastly fought the battles of the society in and out of court. A legal career of unusual promise was sacrificed that he might personally assume, without thought of remuneration, the direction of this important work. Personal attacks were sometimes launched against him by those whose training and position in society should have made them co-workers, because they failed to appreciate the scope of what he had set out to do. Newspapers, with half-truths at their disposal, published misleading articles about him and the society which he represented. The theatre and dance hall managers, the saloon keepers, the tong leaders of Chinatown, and the citizens of the underworld, were as one in fighting with every conceivable weapon the attempts which he made to rescue children from sordid conditions. But Mr. Gerry saw further than they did. He realized that the child was the heart of the nation " and in the chain of national circumstances a neglected, ill-treated, underfed, inefficient, or defective child may easily be the weakest link." Fortunately, many who at first disparaged his work, learned to appreciate and heartily support it.

Elbridge T. Gerry came of sterling American stock. His grandfather, Elbridge Gerry, a Colonial patriot and statesman, was a member of the Continental Congress, a signer of the Declaration of Independence, Governor of Massachusetts, and Vice-President of the United States under President Madison. He was a man of fearless independence who stood by his own convictions and did not hesitate to assert himself for what he thought to be right at whatever the cost in personal popularity.   Thomas R. Gerry was the son of this staunch American and the father of Elbridge T., who was born on Christmas day, 1837.   The mother of the latter was Hannah G., the youngest daughter of Peter P. Goelet.

The Gerrys were possessed of considerable fortune and gave young Elbridge every educational advantage.   At the age of twenty he had graduated from Columbia University and a year later received his master's degree from the institution.   He was a most thorough student and so proficient in Latin that he made a comprehensive study of Roman law.   On graduation, he began the study of law, and on being admitted to the bar, quickly won distinction in his profession.   His practice was extensive and he was extraordinarily successful in the many prominent civil and criminal actions in which he appeared. He gathered in his beautiful Fifth Avenue home a law library of over 30,000 volumes, which constitutes one of the finest private collections of law books in America.

His marked success in his professional work attracted no little attention.   At the age of thirty he was a member of the New York State Constitutional Convention, in which he served on the pardon committee.   In 1886, he was appointed chairman of the New York State Committee on Capital Punishment, which decided upon electrocution as the most humane method of executing

persons guilty of capital crimes. The legislature
accepted the report of the committee and sub-
stituted electrocution in place of hanging. During the celebration of the centennial of the inauguration of George Washington, he served as
the chairman of the Executive Committee. In
1892, he was Chairman of a Commission to consider the best method of dealing with the insane
of New York State. The report submitted was
very complete and became a valuable addition to
the literature on this subject.

Many of those who have long admired Mr.
Gerry's contribution to the cause of child protection are not aware of the fact that he was one of
Henry Bergh's staunchest supporters and most
loyal friends during the latter's pioneer work for
animal protection. Mr. Bergh was delighted to
secure the services of so talented an attorney as
counsel for the American Society for the Prevention of Cruelty to Animals, thus relieving him of
its ever growing legal work. The announcement
of the acquisition of this valuable recruit was
made by him in the fifth annual report of the
society, published in 1871.

From 1870, until Mr. Bergh's death in 1888,
Mr. Gerry prepared all the bills that were introduced at the request of the society at Albany or
Washington. He appeared many times before
legislative committees and by virtue of the legal
knowledge and the strength of his arguments

SENATOR PETER G. GERRY
First Vice-President of The American Humane Association

won important legislation, which, during the subsequent years, has been of the greatest value in
suppressing cruelty.   At the time Mr. Bergh
was restrained by injunction from making ar-
rests of butchers for their cruel methods in
slaughtering hogs, his counsel prepared a brief
citing the legal status of animals from the
earliest recorded history down to the present day.
It was the most exhaustive treatment of the subject ever prepared and was so masterfully drawn
that the injunction was dissolved.[1]   On many
other occasions the society had reason for self-
congratulation that this clear-sighted, aggressive
young attorney was directing its legal department.   At this time, more than at any later date,
precedents were being established on which the
effective interpretation of anticruelty laws now
hinges.

Mr. Bergh was fully cognizant of the part
Mr. Gerry was taking in strengthening the legal
position of animal protection, and paid him the
following compliment in the report of the American Society for the Prevention of Cruelty to
Animals, for 1873:   " To his eminent professional abilities, and devotion to this God-approv-
ing work of defending the defenseless, the society
and its cause owe a debt inappreciable in dollars.
I think that if I had been skeptical of the eternal

---

[1] The Hog Slaughterer's Injunction, Davis vs. American Society
for the Prevention of Cruelty to Animals.

presence of an overruling Providence in the affairs of this world, my repeated experience in the progress of this work would alone suffice to extinguish all doubt.   How often, during its inception and development, have the dark clouds which lowered over my path suddenly and most unexpectedly opened and the aid and support so coveted, the lack of which rendered me for the time so despondent, have come.   I regard this excellent gentleman as a signal manifestation of the Divine Sovereignty to which I allude.   Not only has his prudent and sagacious counsel prevented or parried harm, but by his eloquent and astute advocacy of the rights of the society before the judicial tribunal of the state, he has in some instances affirmed its powers, and preserved to its treasury that material element of its success."

At this time the society presented Mr. Gerry with a loving cup suitably inscribed.   In 1875, Mr. Bergh caused a gold badge to be prepared and presented to Mr. Gerry, who wore it quite constantly for many years.   In acknowledging the gift he wrote: " I trust you will convey to them (directors) my sincere appreciation of the gift and that you will assure them how I appreciate most a decoration and a badge, which, like the cross of the Great Emperor, no money could buy and the privilege of wearing which was itself the patent of nobility."

Mr. Gerry continued actively as counsel of the American Society for the Prevention of Cruelty to Animals until the death of Mr. Bergh in 1888, and remained as one of its vice-presidents until 1899. On his retirement from active participation in its legal work, the directors wrote of him in their records: " Without reward of any kind, he was ever ready to lend his brilliant attainments in behalf of the suffering and helpless, no matter to what life they belonged."

Important, however, as Mr. Gerry's services were in the interest of animal protection, his fame in the field of humanitarian endeavor rests chiefly on his achievements in child rescue work. His part in the formation of the first society for the prevention of cruelty to children, in 1874, was a big one, but at that time he scarcely perceived that he was laying the foundation of a life work. This revelation was to be borne in upon him during the next few years as he studied the possibilities of such an organization and sensed its need for strong leadership. One with so keen an intuition and deep-seated humanitarian impulses could not long continue to take merely a passive or secondary interest in its development.

It was in 1873 that Mrs. Etta Angell Wheeler, a social worker in the New York slums, first learned of the sad plight of the child whose rescue was to bring about the formation of the first society for child protection in the world. For

several months she sought means to remove her
from the clutches of brutal foster parents who
beat her with a whip of twisted leather thongs
until her diminutive body was a mass of cuts and
bruises. The police, the charities, even the courts
offered no method of relief. She " had more than
once been tempted," Mrs. Wheeler wrote, in
after years, " to apply to the Society for the Prevention of Cruelty to Animals, but had lacked
the courage to do what seemed absurd. However, when, on the following Tuesday, a niece
said: ' You are so troubled over that abused
child, why not go to Mr. Bergh? She is a little
animal surely.' I said at once, ' I will go.'
Within an hour I was at the society's rooms.
Mr. Bergh was in his office and listened to my
recital most courteously but with a slight air of
amusement that such an appeal should be made
there. In the end he said: ' The case interests
me much, but very definite testimony is needed
to warrant interference between a child and those
claiming guardianship. Will you not send me a
statement that, at my leisure, I may judge the
weight of the evidence and may also have time to
consider if this society should interfere? I
promise to consider the case carefully.' " [2]

The statement was prepared promptly, and
on April 9, 1874, forty-eight hours after the interview, the child was brought before Judge Law-

---

[2] The Story of Mary Ellen, The American Humane Association.

rence, of the Supreme Court. Jacob Riis, who
was a spectator, that day in court, described the
scene later in a magazine article, which is worthy
of preservation:

" I was in a court room full of men with pale,
stern looks. I saw a child brought in, carried in
a horse blanket, at the sight of which men wept
aloud. I saw it laid at the feet of the judge, who
turned his face away, and in the stillness of that
court room I heard a voice raised claiming for
that child the protection men had denied it, in the
name of the homeless cur on the streets. And I
heard the story of little Mary Ellen told again,
that stirred the soul of a city and roused the conscience of a world that had forgotten. The sweet-
faced missionary who found Mary Ellen was
there, wife of a newspaper man—happy augury;
where the gospel of faith and the gospel of facts
join hands the world moves. She told how the
poor consumptive, in the dark tenement, at
whose bedside she daily read the Bible, could not
die in peace while ' The child they called Mary
Ellen ' was beaten and tortured in the next flat;
and how on weary feet she went from door to
door of the powerful, vainly begging mercy for
it and peace for her dying friend. The police
told her to furnish evidence, to prove crime, or
they could not move; the Societies said, ' Bring
the child to us legally and we will see; till then
we can do nothing;' the charitable said, ' It is

dangerous to interfere between parent and child; better let it alone;' and the judges said it was even so; it was for them to see that men walked in the way laid down, not to find it—until her woman's heart rebelled against it all, and she sought the great friend of dumb brutes, who made a way.

" ' The child is an animal,' he said. ' If there is no justice for it as a human being, it shall at least have the rights of the cur in the street. It shall not be abused.'

" And as I looked I knew I was where the first chapter of the children's rights was written under warrant of that made for the dog; for from that dingy court room, whence a wicked woman went to jail, thirty years ago, came forth The New York Society for the Prevention of Cruelty to Children, with all it has meant to the world's life. It is quickening its pulse in this day in lands and among peoples who never spoke the name of my city and Mary Ellen's." [3]

On leaving the court room Mrs. Wheeler paused to thank Mr. Bergh for his assistance and ask " If there could not be a society for the prevention of cruelty to children which should do for abused children what was being so well done for animals? He took my hand and said very

---

[3] Address, " Sister Societies Abroad," by E. Fellows Jenkins, delivered at 30th Annual Meeting of The American Humane Association.

emphatically: ' There shall be one.' " The existence to-day of several hundred such organizations testifies how well this promise was kept.

New York was greatly stirred by the details
of this case, which were fully reported in the
papers. Several similar cases were brought to
the society for solution. Action of some sort was
necessary. With characteristic vigor Mr. Bergh
began to sound out public opinion regarding the
formation of such a society. The original peti-
tion, or " Inspiration," drawn by him is now one
of the prized documents of the New York Society
for the Prevention of Cruelty to Children. It
bears the signatures of Henry Bergh, Elbridge
T. Gerry, John D. Wright and other prominent
persons. The society was instituted December
15, 1874. Mr. Gerry was requested to draw up
the incorporation papers and arrange for its charter under the name of the New York Society for
the Prevention of Cruelty to Children, which was
finally obtained in 1875.

In the ninth report of the American Society
for the Prevention of Cruelty to Animals, published the same year, Mr. Bergh wrote: " It is
with infinite satisfaction that I report the formation of a Society for the Prevention of Cruelty
to Children. And it will afford you, likewise, I
am certain, an equal share of pleasure to know
that to this society is due, in a great degree, the
consummation of this important fact. That the

sad case of ' little Mary Ellen,' which Mr. Gerry
and others so wisely conducted to a happy result
was the nucleus of its creation there is little
doubt; and that the suffering of that little frac-
tion of humanity inspired the kind-hearted Mr.
John D. Wright to take the leading part in its
formation and usefulness is also true. Nor, while
alluding to the incidents, should I fail to make
mention that to Mrs. Charles C. Wheeler are due
the honor and credit of first calling my attention
to the deplorable condition of that child. Mr.
Gerry has prepared an act of incorporation,
which includes many of our most eminent and
humane citizens, and it has already been presented to the legislature."

The society quickly became a power in New
York City, where it has afforded more than a
million children the benefit of its legal protection. Other cities adopted the idea. Its possibilities so appealed to Frederick A. Agnew, of
England, who was visiting in America, that on
his return, he organized a society, in Liverpool, in
1882. The National Society for the Prevention
of Cruelty to Children, with offices in London,
which has representatives stationed in all the important centers of Great Britain, was a direct
outgrowth, in 1884. For more than twenty years
Rev. Benjamin Waugh was the guiding and
directing spirit of this organization. The movement has also taken deep root on the Continent

Headquarters of the New York Society for Prevention of Cruelty to Children, Fifth Avenue, New York

of Europe and in other parts of the world. Since
the parent society was founded in 1875, more
than 500 other similar organizations have been
created.

Before the organization of the New York
society, the abused child had practically no pro-
tector, as the case of " Mary Ellen " clearly
showed. Under the theory of the law the state
had the obligation placed upon it to protect the
child " in person and property and in its opportunity for life, liberty and the pursuit of happi-
ness," but with no special organization or department of government to see that these rights were
enforced the lot of thousands of children beg-
gared description. A vivid picture of these conditions is drawn by President Gerry in the tenth
report of the New York society:

" Impecunious parents drove them from their
miserable homes at all hours of the day and night
to beg and steal. They were trained as acrobats
at the risk of life and limb, and beaten cruelly if
they failed. They were sent at night to procure
liquor for parents too drunk to venture themselves into the streets. They were drilled in
juvenile operas and song and dance variety business until their voices were cracked, their growth
stunted, and their health permanently ruined by
exposure and want of rest. Numbers of young
Italians were imported by *padroni* under promises of a speedy return, and then sent out on the

streets to play on musical instruments, to peddle
flowers and small wares to the passers-by and too
often as a cover for immorality. Their surroundings were those of vice, profanity, and obscenity.
Their only amusements were the dance halls, the
cheap theatres, and museums and saloons. Their
acquaintances were those hardened in sin, and
both boys and girls soon became adepts in crime,
and entered unhesitatingly on the downward
path. Beaten and abused at home, treated worse
than animals, no other result could be expected.
In the prisons, to which sooner or later these unhappy children gravitated, there was no separation of them from hardened criminals. Their
previous education in vice rendered them
apt scholars in the school of crime, and they
ripened into criminals as they advanced in years."

Those acquainted with conditions in New
York before the advent of the society have
stated that there were ten thousand homeless
boys roaming the streets by day and taking what
scant shelter they could find at night. The
wharves were overrun with them. The public
manifested no interest in them unless to search
them out for committing crime.

Nearly a half century of concentrated effort has witnessed the gradual disappearance of
many of the more open and glaring phases of
cruelty to children. They are only kept to a
minimum by the eternal vigilance of trained and

experienced agents. Behind closed doors cruel persons still vent their unrestrained rage on little children. It is but a short time since a child was brought to the society's shelter, whose body bore one hundred and eleven welts. " His teeth were broken and his eye nearly torn from its socket. The boy's own father had beaten him with the buckle of a harness trace until, as the man said, ' the kid couldn't stand up.' The poor little chap managed to crawl into a dark cellar, where his piteous moans aroused a neighbor, who notified the society."

Mr. John D. Wright, a wealthy New York Quaker, consented to serve as the society's first President. Although well on in years, he gave careful thought and attention to the advancement of the organization until his death in 1879. At that time Elbridge T. Gerry was unanimously elected to succeed him. From the day when Mrs. Wheeler first came to the office of Mr. Bergh to ask for his assistance in the case of Mary Ellen, Mr. Gerry had been in most intimate touch with the progress of the child saving movement. During Mr. Wright's presidency, Mr. Gerry handled the legal work as its official counsel. The corporate powers conferred upon it to enforce the laws and the enactment of statutes to protect the children were the product of his labor. He knew the intricacies of its work in every aspect and the problems that confronted its management. Who else could so completely fill the requirements needed to insure the permanency of the society and successfully carry out its program? Mr. Gerry faced these facts and unhesitatingly assumed the responsibility entailed in blazing the untrodden trail of child protection. Gradually the burden became so exacting that he was obliged to give up his general law practice and devote all of his energy to this work. For nineteen years of the ripest period of his life he gave himself unreservedly to the arduous labor of developing the society's protection powers. It became a holy mission which gripped his waking and sleeping hours. When others might have been discouraged and inclined to give up the struggle for the little ones who had no one else to champion their cause, he took hold with new vigor and determination and by sheer personal force achieved a mighty victory for humanity.

President Gerry stoutly supported the provision of the law which requires that children be sent to institutions of their own religious faith, believing that the parental faith of the child should not be interfered with if it became necessary to take it from its home for its protection and place it in a public institution. He therefore stressed time and again the importance of thorough religious teaching of the faith of the parent so that the children should have the advantage of that important factor in home train-

COLONEL ERNEST K. COULTER
*General Manager, the New York Society for
the Prevention of Cruelty to Children*

ing, which was, in his opinion, the most essential part of child education.

He always insisted, from the formative days of the society, that child rescue work was an exclusive task and must not be confused with other phases of child welfare. "Our societies for the prevention of cruelty to children," he once said, " were instituted for the express purpose, and for no other, of applying the arm of the law to the protection of the helpless. Their duty was to see that the law, which was potent in its terms, was not left to become inert and paralyzed for want of applications to its object."

On another occasion he summarized the work of the society as he considered it should be conducted. " First, it receives on commitment at its own expense by and subject to the courts all children charged with commission of crime who otherwise would be sent to the city prison. Second, it receives by and subject to the order of the courts, children who are themselves the unhappy victims of physical violence, or who are held as witnesses pending the criminal prosecution of the cruelist.

" The importance of these two subjects will be seen at a glance. But for the society, children arrested for any offense, great or trivial, would be subject to confinement in a penal institution, whether innocent or guilty, until the issue was finally determined. Again, children who are victims of physical violence not only frequently require medical care and attention, but a careful examination is often directed by order of the court, to determine the truth of their story, and to corroborate their evidence against the offender.   All such examinations are made by skilled physicians assisted by a competent nurse, with every facility afforded by the best hospitals in the land."

The children's shelter, as the institution for the temporary care of children is commonly called, was developed at an early date by societies for the prevention of cruelty to children. The New York society equipped its first building in 1880.   Children's shelters are in no sense of the word reform schools or orphanages, though they are in many instances the clearing house for such institutions.   They afford the only satisfactory method of safeguarding young witnesses from the interference of those who would tamper with their testimony and thus defeat the ends of justice.   Another valuable feature of shelters is the means they afford for the immediate relief of sufferers.   They are open night and day to receive them.   Deserted mothers, with families of little ones; children lost on the streets, or made helpless by accident, or by the cruelty of one or both parents; boys who have wandered away to become youthful tramps; young girls who have fallen into bad company; these and many others find such shelters temporary abiding places, where they are safe from harm and their immediate wants can receive attention. Until recently the children's shelter was exclusively an agency of child protective societies, but with the coming of the juvenile court some cities have established similar refuges because there was no society for the prevention of cruelty to children in the place or because such society was comparatively inactive.

The counsel of the New York society is specially deputized by the Attorney General of the state and by the district attorney to appear in cases involving children. From the beginning the society has been remarkably successful in its prosecutions. Some years ago the New York State Board of Charities attempted to gain control over the society on the theory that it was a charity. The matter was carried to the Court of Appeals by President Gerry, which found (161 N. Y. Reports, page 233) adversely to the Board. A further unsuccessful attempt was made during the last Constitutional Convention. The court held the society to be an arm of the law, which was to be used in criminal cases affecting children, instead of the ordinary police, who are overburdened with crimes involving adults.

During the many stormy years President Gerry was actively at the helm, hundreds of in-

teresting cases were handled by the society.   In
some of them the trail of evidence led across the
continent.   In not a few instances the efforts of
the New York society to gain necessary facts or
secure possession of a child in a distant city
aroused so much local interest that a society was
formed with the one in New York as a model.

The prosecutions of the *padroni* system
stretched out across the sea to Italy.   Among
the most important of these cases was one
brought against Ancarola, who, in 1879,
brought seven Italian children to America for
use as street musicians.   The alertness of the
society soon uncovered the evidence, and the
offender was brought to trial before the United
States Court.   Ancarola was convicted and,
after a bitter fight, the decision was upheld by
the United States Court.   A sentence of five
years meted out to the defendant helped materially to bring this disgraceful practice to an
end.

The law placed on the New York statute
books, through the personal efforts of President
Gerry, to regulate the appearance of children in
public performances has always been a difficult
one to enforce.   Little did the theatre-going
crowds appreciate the tragedies hidden in the
hearts and lives of the child actors who afforded
them brief amusement.   The society has always
insisted on an impartial and exact application

of the law in such cases, and has thereby prevented many young lives from being permanently ruined. The rulings laid down by it have at times been most unpopular with the general public, but time and experience have gradually shown the need for the regulations imposed, and that the policy of the society in such matters was sound. It was necessary to educate the community to new standards in many matters concerning children. Mr. Gerry was always patient, persistent and humane, although at times an aggressive educator.

At all times Elbridge T. Gerry kept a firm hand upon the detail work of his society. In this way he inspired his assistants to give their best efforts to their respective tasks. The bigger problems of management and policy received the careful scrutiny of a judicial mind. The society was not organized to cope with a passing evil, but one that could only be curbed by everlasting vigilance and application. Mr. Gerry knew this better than his critics and planned for permanency and stability. On his retirement from the presidency in 1899 he left an organization that was the largest of its kind in the world and one which even opponents acknowledged was efficient and practical.

The state and the national humane movements have profited largely by his personal service. In 1888, he served as President of The

American Humane Association. Under its present administration he has taken the greatest interest in its development. He was the leading spirit in the formation of the Convention of Societies for the Prevention of Cruelty to Children and Animals in New York State. This was the first state organization of independent societies that would act as a unit in advancing or opposing legislation. He was elected its first President in 1890 and held the office for thirteen years. It has been at times very largely dependent upon his generosity for its financial support.

While the bulk of President Gerry's time was given for years to humane work, reference has already been made to public positions filled by him. Other public duties included: Governor New York Hospital (1878-1912); Trustee General Theological Seminary P. E. Church (1877-1913); Trustee American Museum of Natural History (1895-1902); President of the Chi Psi Fraternity and Commodore of the New York Yacht Club (1886-1893). In 1910, he received the degree of LL. D. from Nashotah.

The younger son, Hon. Peter Goelet Gerry, United States Senator from Rhode Island, has rendered excellent service to the humane cause. His unfailing courtesy and his abiding sympathy for those that suffer, whether found in the human or sub-human families, have won for him a large circle of friends among humanitarians. For a number of years he has been the First Vice-President of The American Humane Association, and has the liveliest concern and interest in its numerous activities.

On Mr. Elbridge T. Gerry's retirement from the Presidency of the New York Society in 1899, he was succeeded by Hon. Vernon M. Davis, at the time foremost at the bar as a brilliant and fearless prosecuting officer in the criminal courts of New York. Judge Davis occupied the office of President until 1903, retiring to go on the Bench of the New York Supreme Court. He was succeeded by Mr. John D. Lindsay, a prominent member of the New York bar, who in turn was followed by Hon. M. Linn Bruce, who had previously been Lieutenant Governor of New York State and a Justice of the Supreme Court. President Bruce brought to his office unquestioned abilities, and still further advanced the efficiency and scope of the New York Children's Society.

At the time the New York Society for the Prevention of Cruelty to Children was formed in 1874, Mr. E. Fellows Jenkins, who had been the very active Superintendent of the American Society for the Prevention of Cruelty to Animals since 1868, was proposed by Mr. Bergh as its secretary and superintendent. He continued to hold that position until his resignation in 1909.

At the close of 1914, Col. Ernest K. Coulter was chosen to fill the superintendency left vacant by the death of the late Mr. Thomas D. Walsh, who succeeded Mr. Jenkins. The choice was a most fortunate one. Col. Coulter was one of the organizers of the New York Children's Court and its clerk for ten years. In that way he had opportunity to study thoroughly the methods and the traditions of the society whose cases were daily before the court. As the founder of the Big Brother Movement he had lectured from coast to coast, and had become probably as well known personally to those interested in child protection as any man in America. His book " The Children in the Shadow " has had great popularity, and has been instrumental in moulding social thought. Col. Coulter has had extensive newspaper experience, and is a member of the New York bar. During the war with Germany he gave up his position to serve in the American Army. He was mustered out with the rank of Lieut. Colonel, and immediately resumed his connection with the children's society under the title of General Manager.

GEORGE T. ANGELL

Founder and President Massachusetts Society for the
Prevention of Cruelty to Animals, 1868 to 1909

Chapter IV

GEORGE T. ANGELL: THE APOSTLE OF HUMANE EDUCATION

WHILE George Thorndike Angell was the first to develop the full possibilities of humane education and wrote and spoke almost constantly in its behalf, it should not be forgotten that he was the founder and President of The Massachusetts Society for the Prevention of Cruelty to Animals, one of the earliest organizations of its kind, which has done a very practical and efficient work for animal protection. In addition, he was president of The American Humane Education Society, which was created for the distribution of humane literature and the diffusion of humane ideals and propaganda. No person could have been more devoted to the cause which he advocated than Mr. Angell. He was consistent in his efforts and never neglected an opportunity to help dumb animals and to spread humane education.

No one else has inspired the writing and caused the distribution of so many pages of humane literature. In the field of animal protection he shares with Henry Bergh the title of pioneer.   It detracts in no whit from the glory of either that they pursued different methods to achieve their desired ends.   Although they began their crusades at practically the same time there is no evidence that they consulted one another to any extent or had more than a slight acquaintance.   Each was a law unto himself. Bergh was distant and reserved, with few close personal friends.   Angell was warm and enthusiastic, with multitudes of warm friends everywhere.

Mr. Angell was born at Southbridge, Worcester County, Mass., June 5, 1823.   He died in Boston, March 16, 1909.   His life was full of stirring events.   Near its close he once said: " I have succeeded in everything I have tried to do."   This was not the boast of an egotist but the candid expression of an optimist. He believed his life was divinely guided.   This led him to view all his undertakings with a confidence of fulfilment that men with less faith never would have undertaken.   Every task was approached through prayer, though he was not narrow or fanatical in his religious attitude. He worked in closest harmony with people of all faiths and secured their warmest cooperation in forwarding his humane mission.

With the acumen of a modern advertising specialist, he capitalized his personality.   He kept his name before the masses by circulating *Our Dumb Animals* among those who moulded public opinion. Each issue reached every newspaper office in America, every college president, each member of Congress, and, within Massachusetts, every clergyman, lawyer, judge, and state legislator, besides the police force of Boston and thousands of school children scattered throughout America. Whether he was regarded as a fanatic or revered as a leader in a great moral movement, his name came to stand for " animal protection " and " humane education."

But Mr. Angell did not limit his propaganda to the printed page. He was a convincing speaker and understood fully the art of public address. The pulpit, the lyceum, the stage, the school room, the grange platform, even the assemblies in penitentiary or prison, afforded him the opportunity to reach thousands, who helped to pass on the lessons of kindness and mercy. No one has to his credit the founding of so many animal protective societies, or has so influenced the trend of constructive humane thought as George Thorndike Angell, the Humane Educator.

It is a strange coincidence that at about the time Henry Bergh reached his decision to devote his life to animal protection, Mr. Angell drew a will, in 1864, in which the following paragraph appeared:

" It has long been my opinion, that there is much wrong in the treatment of domestic animals; that they are too often overworked, overpunished, and, particularly in winter and in times of scarcity, underfed. All these I think great wrongs, particularly the last; and it is my earnest wish to do something towards awakening public sentiment on this subject; the more so, because these animals have no power of complaint, or adequate human protection, against those who are disposed to do them injury. I do therefore direct that all the remainder of my property not herein before disposed of shall, within two years after the decease of my mother and myself, or the survivor, be expended by my trustees in circulating in common schools, Sabbath schools, or other schools, or otherwise, in such manner as my trustees shall deem best, such books, tracts, or pamphlets as in their judgment will tend most to impress upon the minds of youth their duty towards those domestic animals which God may make dependent upon them."

Both of these knights of humanity were born in 1823; Bergh in a home of wealth, with every opportunity for a great commercial career; Angell in a Baptist parsonage in a little Massachusetts town. The boyhood of each was marked with a deep love for animals and an abiding sense of justice. Mr. Angell was born with no silver spoon. His father, Rev. George Angell,

died when he was only four years old. He had
been a much loved pastor, but he left his son
George little in a material way. Mrs. Angell
was the daughter of Paul Thorndike. At the
time of her marriage she was teaching school,
and was obliged to resume such work on the
death of her husband. Her devotion was a wonderful inspiration to George, who often declared
" No man ever had a better mother." Much of
his boyhood was spent among relatives in small
New England towns. At fourteen he entered
a Boston drygoods store, where he remained two
years. His mother was determined that he
should receive a college education. After a brief
preparatory period he matriculated at Brown
University in 1842, but because of the expense
transferred to Dartmouth, from which he graduated with the class of 1846. His mother had
helped him as she could, but the bulk of the cost
of his education he had earned by teaching
school.

A wealthy relative in Salem soon offered him
a chance to study law in his office. A position
was secured as a teacher in the Boston public
schools, which not only provided his expenses,
but enabled him to partially support his mother,
pay off a college debt of $300, and have a
bank account of $1200 at the end of three
years. In 1851 he was admitted to the bar. For
a number of years he enjoyed successful part-

nerships with several prominent Boston attorneys, including Samuel E. Sewall, an able lawyer and a prominent abolitionist. This last connection continued for fourteen years and was a most happy and prosperous one. In order to gain more time for his public life, it was voluntarily dissolved, and Mr. Angell took in a junior partner. At the end of nine years he gave up professional work entirely to devote his attention to the service of the human and sub-human sufferers. As an attorney, Mr. Angell was successful in court work, but on account of his health he preferred to build up an office practice. His Yankee shrewdness and unfailing integrity were great factors in advancing the interests of his clients. One of the best evidences of his ability was the fact that in a little less than twenty years he was able to build up a fortune sufficiently large to enable him to withdraw from his profession and devote himself entirely to philanthropic efforts.

He had often been shocked by acts of cruelty to animals so prevalent in the period preceding the organization of anticruelty societies. But there was no law under which the cruelist could be brought to justice. It required a flagrant act of cruelty within his own state to focus attention on the evil sufficiently to arouse the slumbering flame of an outraged conscience. In his " Autobiography " he describes a few of the wrongs that were then prevalent in every state in the Union.

" Calves taken from their mothers when too young to eat hay were carted through our streets and lay in heaps at the cattle-markets, tied, and piled on each other like sticks of wood; and they were bled several times before they were killed, to make their flesh look whiter and more delicate.   Sheep, from which their fleeces had been taken, stood, in cold weather, about the slaughter-yards shivering for days before they were killed.   Nothing had been done to lessen the horrors of cattle transportation.   Old horses, long past service, were whipped up and down the streets of Brighton, and sometimes sold for thirty-seven and a half cents each.   Worn-out and aged horses, dogs, and other animals were ignorantly and thoughtlessly killed, in ways most brutal.   A man in my town near Boston, who had mortgaged his stock of cattle to another, quarrelled with him, locked the stable doors, and starved them all to death in their stalls to prevent his getting his pay.   There was no law in Massachusetts to punish him! "

The culminating act was a horse race between Brighton and Worcester, on Washington's birthday, 1868, in which two of the finest horses were driven to death.   Mr. Angell said: " I had heard that Mr. Bergh had started a society in New York and I determined that somebody must take hold of this business, and I might as well as anybody." Then occurred one of the characteristic acts of his life. He wrote a letter to the *Boston Advertiser* in which he recounted the details of the race and called upon those who were interested to join him in forming a society for the prevention of cruelty to animals.

The following morning, February 26, 1868, a number of distinguished people called upon him and offered their cooperation. Among them was Mrs. William Appleton, a woman of influence and position. She had already seen Mr. Bergh and had the signatures of some ninety or more of her influential friends, who had agreed to become patrons of such an organization.

Mr. Angell acutely realized that his opportunity had come to right the wrongs he had seen committed upon his speechless friends. Letters were addressed to the papers calling for members and funds. The act of incorporation, which Mrs. Appleton had already submitted to the Speaker of the Massachusetts House of Representatives, was redrafted, though this influential personage assured him that there was no chance of a charter being granted. Mr. Angell, however, had so aroused public sentiment that, on March 23, 1868, before the close of the session, the charter was voted.

The following day the Boston papers con-

George T. Angell Memorial Hospital, Boston

tained a call for a meeting to organize the society. On the 31st of March, 1868, about forty persons gathered in Mr. Angell's law office, adopted the constitution and by-laws which he had drawn, and elected him President. He held the office continuously and with ever increasing effectiveness until his death on March 16, 1909. The Board of Directors contained the names of some of Boston's foremost citizens. At the close of the meeting Mr. Angell and the newly elected Secretary, Mr. Russell Sturgis, Jr., withdrew into a private office and together knelt and prayed for God's blessing on the enterprise, a practice that Mr. Angell always followed in beginning all of the work that was to make his name a household word.

As with the New York society, the next step was to lay the foundation of a code of laws under which the society should have power to apprehend those guilty of wrongdoing against the lower animals. Mr. Angell drafted a law, and by the use of newspaper publicity and extensive correspondence, secured favorable action by the legislature on May 14, 1868. "It was already clear to my mind," wrote Mr. Angell, "that I was entering upon my life work; and my plans reached far beyond anything that I could learn had been thus far undertaken." He not only recognized the need of a state-wide prosecuting agency, but also realized the importance of an

7

educational program that would remove the source of cruelty.

While the legislature was considering the novel bill that had been presented to it by Mr. Angell, he was busily planning how his society would enforce it when it became available. Members were needed for moral and financial support. It was while he was trying to devise some satisfactory scheme for canvassing the city that one of the " inspirations " occurred which he regarded as providential.

Meeting by chance a prominent police official, he asked where the canvassers could be obtained. " Borrow some of the police," was his suggestion. The idea was charged with possibilities. Permission was quickly obtained from the necessary officials and seventeen finely groomed policemen were detailed to Mr. Angell for three weeks. The response was prompt and gave the society 1200 of the 1600 members and put about $13,000 in its treasury. Another incident in this campaign which Mr. Angell regarded as providential was the fact that the opposition candidate for mayor was canvassed among the last. Had he known sooner what was going on, the policemen would never have been permitted to finish their work.

Humane history was being made rapidly in old Boston. Six days after the passage of the anticruelty law, Mr. Angell called his directors together and proposed the publication of a monthly magazine which should be widely circulated in behalf of humane education. The idea was acceptable to them. " How many will you print? "

" Two hundred thousand," was the immediate reply.

" How much will it cost? "

" Between two and three thousand dollars."

It is not difficult to imagine that the conservative business men on the directorate were " startled." It was a bold move, but time has well established its wisdom. Accordingly, on June 2, 1868, appeared the first edition of *Our Dumb Animals,* the pioneer magazine of its class in the world. Since that date it has never missed a month when its messages of good will to animals have not been scattered widely throughout the nation and in many foreign countries as well. The value of the publication to the Massachusetts Society for the Prevention of Cruelty to Animals and later to The American Humane Education Society, was often referred to by Mr. Angell in later years. Not only did it teach many valuable lessons of kindness, which cannot be measured in money, but it proved a most essential aid in building up the society's membership and inducing persons to make their wills in favor of the society. The distribution was most carefully considered from both standpoints. The editions ran from 50,000 to 100,000 or more copies.

But to go back to that first edition of 200,000 copies. Mr. Angell sought to have the police distribute the magazine from house to house, much as they had canvassed the city for memberships. When he broached the matter to the authorities he was told that the opposition candidate for mayor had caused a resolution to be passed by the City Council forbidding the use of the police for any private or corporate enterprise. As Mr. Angell was leaving the Mayor's office he discovered a friend who, on hearing of the situation, agreed to secure the approval of the aldermen. He was as good as his word, and the Boston police force delivered more than 30,000 copies of *Our Dumb Animals* without any charge whatever to the society. The same plan was adopted for handling the distribution in other cities. It was another one of the " providential " situations which seemed to follow Mr. Angell through life.

The Massachusetts Society for the Prevention of Cruelty to Animals was now fully organized and prosecuting agents were appointed for Boston and other cities of the state. The first case prosecuted was for overloading a team of horses. The court ruled the case out. Mr. Angell reviewed the evidence in the *Boston Transcript* and so clearly set forth the evidence governing the overloading of animals that Bishop included it in his " Statutory Crimes." This statement is still accepted as sound law.

By the end of the first year of the society's existence Mr. Angell had broken down in health from overwork and left for a rest in Europe, in the Spring of 1869. While abroad he became a warm friend of John Colam, the secretary of the Royal Society for the Prevention of Cruelty to Animals, of London, England. His glowing account of the value of an official magazine, such as his society had in *Our Dumb Animals,* moved the English society to begin the publication of *The Animal World,* a name partially suggested by Mr. Angell. Its initial number was published in October, 1869. It is the second oldest magazine devoted to animal protection. By invitation, he addressed a meeting at the home of Miss Coutts, later Baroness Burdett-Coutts, then the richest and most philanthropic woman in England. So deeply impressed was she by his plea for humane education that she consented to head the ladies' humane education committee of the English society. Mr. Angell had the pleasure of attending a meeting of the French Society for the Prevention of Cruelty to Animals, in Paris, and was the only American delegate at a World's International Congress of Animal Protective Societies held in Zurich.

During the fifteen months Mr. Angell was

abroad, he wrote regularly for *Our Dumb Animals* and a glance through its old files gives some very interesting memoirs of his trip.   His suggestion that the Royal Society offer a series of prizes to the pupils of the London schools for the best essays on kindness to animals was tried out with excellent results.   Mr. Angell became a warm advocate of this method of stimulating interest in the humane cause on his return to America, and during his long connection with the society distributed several thousand dollars in various prize competitions.

Mr. Angell had hardly time to adjust himself to the affairs of his society on his return to Boston, in 1870, before he was sought by Hon. John C. Dore, of Chicago, Ill., to go to that city to aid the movement that had been started there. The invitation was accepted and Mr. Angell arrived in Chicago, October 30th.   At the end of six months of the hardest work, during which time he gave his services and paid out six hundred dollars of his own money, he had the pleasure of seeing the Illinois Humane Society well established with Edwin Lee Brown as its first president.

This was the beginning of a series of humane missionary journeys through the states, as far West as Dakota and South to New Orleans, that were to continue as long as his health would permit him to travel.   Through his counsel, the in-

fluence of his lectures and the compelling power
of his enthusiasm, he probably led to the formation of more societies, large and small, than any
other humanitarian. He always paid his own
expenses and frequently spent considerable sums
from his own purse, as in the case of Chicago, to
insure the formation of a local anticruelty society. In this he was invariably successful,
which was all the reward he asked for himself.
He had the honor of addressing thousands of
people in widely scattered districts and of vastly
different social grades. Legislatures, churches,
colleges, penitentiaries, schools, granges, and
Sunday schools listened intently to his message
of mercy. His lectures made a strong appeal
and the directness and simplicity of his story
went straight to the hearts of the people.

Many interesting anecdotes have been preserved of his speaking tours. One which he relates in his Autobiography will suffice:

"At Brattleboro, Vt., I engaged the town-
hall, agreeing to pay all expenses and for its use,
and had notice given in the schools. The night
of my lecture happened to be one of the hottest
of the season. I went to the hall a quarter of
an hour in advance, and found it not lighted,
only the janitor and half a dozen rough boys.
'Why don't you light the hall?' said I. 'Well,
I thought I'd wait, and see if anybody was
coming,' said he. 'Coming!' said I; 'why,

here's half a dozen boys already.' ' You ain't
going to *lectur* to these boys, are you? ' said he.
' Certainly I am,' said I, ' if nobody else comes.
One of them may be governor of Vermont, one
of these days, for aught I know.' So he lit the
hall, and gradually some hundreds gathered;
and now they have a society in Brattleboro, Vt.,
for the prevention of cruelty to animals."

But not all of his time was spent away from
home. At no time did he lose his grasp on the
affairs of the Massachusetts Society for the Prevention of Cruelty to Animals or its magazine,
Our Dumb Animals. If the society's funds were
low he found ways to increase them. When he
wanted state legislation he drafted it and fought
for its passage. If publicity was needed in order
to combat some atrocious form of cruelty, he
flooded the local papers with its exposure and
condemnation.

He had the satisfaction of seeing live
pigeon shooting abolished by law in the face of
the most violent opposition, at about the time
the sport was being legalized in New York. He
went to Washington and helped secure legislation, not all that was desired, but a step in the
right direction, regulating interstate shipments of
livestock. He had the honor of writing a portion of President Hayes' inaugural address dealing with the transportation of animals. President Garfield received him courteously and

aided his work. In fact, not until he fearlessly denounced the hunting trips of President Roosevelt, that caused the public schools of Washington, D. C., to bar *Our Dumb Animals,* did he have any difficulty in securing recognition from the White House.

A big mile stone in Mr. Angell's life was the creation of the American Band of Mercy, with the help of Rev. Thomas Timmins, of England, who visited Boston during July, 1882. Mr. Timmins had had extensive experience with the English Band of Mercy, originated by Mrs. Smithies, shortly after Mr. Angell's visit to England. Between them the whole plan of the movement was sketched out as it is now followed. This means of reaching the child was a popular one and was quickly taken up. By 1921 there had been 131,688 Bands formed in the United States.

Another great achievement, and the one which Mr. Angell ranked as his greatest, was the founding of The American Humane Education Society, in 1889. It originally had the same directors as The Massachusetts Society for the Prevention of Cruelty to Animals, but with different duties. During the twenty years, or more, that Mr. Angell had been devoting to the subject of cruelty to animals he had conceived that humane education was of greater importance than prosecution. While the Massachusetts

Society had been unable to finance this phase of
its work outside of the state, he had done much
personally.   His new organization had for its
purpose the creation and the distribution of such
propaganda as would be useful to humane workers.   He also proposed to send out organizers to
those communities that could not afford to
finance their own work.   The society has done
and is doing a most meritorious work.   Millions
of pages of literature have been distributed,
much of it entirely free, and several missionaries
are kept in sparsely settled or poor districts to
look after animal protection.   Several of its
workers are colored people, who toil among
their own race.

"Black Beauty" has probably been the most
popular of all the literature published by The
American Humane Education Society.   This
book had a very limited circulation in England,
where it was published some twelve years before
it was brought to the attention of Mr. Angell
by that noble humanitarian, Miss Georgiana
Kendall, of New York.   He at once pronounced
it "The Uncle Tom's Cabin of the Horse" and
set about securing an edition of 100,000 copies.
Before his death he had seen its circulation reach
3,000,000 copies.   It was translated into a number of foreign languages, and made the most
widely read book in the world, outside of the
Bible.   The demand for it continues steadily

from year to year. The whole story has been dramatized for the stage and has been adapted to moving pictures.

Mr. Angell was a great friend of dogs and often fought for their rights before the legislature. He did much to allay the ill-grounded fears of hydrophobia, denounced vivisection, and took active stands against all forms of animal abuse.

Posterity will know him because of the invaluable service he rendered the animal kingdom. He is entitled to be remembered for the other contributions he made to safeguard humanity. At the risk of being much misunderstood, he exposed the general practice followed of adulterating foodstuffs and was among the first to seek legislation to prevent it. His public exposure of the use of a poisonous substance on a newly introduced enamel ware caused the manufacturers to withdraw the product from the market. He pointed out the dangers arising from the use of poisons in the coloring of wall paper. One whole winter was spent in Washington in an attempt to have Congress pass a law against poisonous adulterations. His own state ultimately did so and his nation-wide fight undoubtedly did much to bring about the present pure food laws.

Early and late he wrote and lectured on crime and advocated the extension of humane educa-

tion as a remedy against it. He was opposed to
war and scarcely an issue of *Our Dumb Animals* appeared without giving space to the desirability of international courts of arbitration.

With the exception of a brief period he acted
as the editor of his magazine. Even towards the
close of his long life, when the ravages of
asthma prevented his going to the office, except
for the annual meetings of his societies, he edited
it from his own home and directed the work of
the two organizations. His last editorial was
written within a few hours of his death. Though
he realized his end was near, because of his difficulty in breathing, he said that " he should live
three years longer to accomplish plans he had in
mind."

The press all over the country, in announcing his death, devoted much space to his memory.
Thirty-eight draught horses were led behind the
hearse bearing the remains of their champion.
Hundreds of Boston's work horses wore black
rosettes as evidence of the affection felt by horse
owners and drivers for the man who demanded
a square deal for beast as well as man. Judged
by the work which he accomplished, George
Thorndike Angell deserves to be ranked among
the greatest humanitarians in the world's history. All agree that his contribution to the
humane cause was a mighty one and that the
benefits of his earnest labors will survive as long

as the world recognizes the principles of humanity.

His lovable nature was a joy and an inspiration. A stranger called at his home shortly before his death, and as he left said to Mrs. Angell: " I felt I could not go home without shaking hands with Mr. Angell. The inspiration I have received from talking with that man will remain throughout life." It was ever so. His heart was where the world could see. He was a fighter for what he believed in, but his methods were clean and open. He inspired confidence and loyalty in his staff by his sincerity and magnanimity. A friend once said of him, " One could not talk with him five minutes without realizing and appreciating his wise judgment."

Mr. Angell married Mrs. Eliza A. Martin, of Nahant, Mass., in 1872. He was very fond of her and depended greatly on her for advice and encouragement. He once declared that she had prolonged his life ten years. Mrs. Angell still lives. She is a most loyal and ardent humanitarian, proud of her privilege of having been permitted to share the labor of her illustrious husband.

The memory of George T. Angell has been preserved to posterity by a magnificent drinking fountain for animals, erected in Boston by the school children of the city. A large Boston public school also bears his name. His crowning memorial was the erection of a great and beautiful building in Boston which houses the two great organizations which he founded and provides hospital treatment for thousands of animals, annually. It is known as The Angell Animal Memorial Hospital.

Shortly after the death of Mr. Angell, a special committee of the two societies which he had founded and developed so wisely, selected Rev. Francis Harold Rowley, D.D., as his successor. In its report the committee stated: " Dr. Rowley is so far a man of the world that his activities have not been confined to a parish or to the pulpit. His interest in the humane movement led him to assume for several years the duties of secretary of The American Humane Association, where he became familiar with the work and established an acquaintance and connection with many of those who are still engaged in it in various parts of the country. He is in touch with other humane workers and movements in our field, and it will especially interest those who hold in respect the memory of Mr. Angell to know that Dr. Rowley was one of his valued friends and one of the few toward whom he looked in his later years as a possible successor."

During the period that Dr. Rowley has been President of the joint societies, they have expanded their work in every direction. It was under his leadership that the beautiful Angell

Memorial Animal Hospital was erected and formally opened, February 25, 1915. The hospital is most modern in its equipment and has ministered to a large number of animals. Another material addition to the equipment of the society was the acquiring of the Nevins Rest and Boarding Farm for Horses, at Methuen, in 1917. The buildings have been altered to meet the demands of the work and the farm put in condition so that a large number of animals may be conveniently handled. The revenue derived from the sale of farm products aids to no small extent in meeting the expenses of the place.

President Rowley has seen a large increase in the revenue of the Massachusetts Society for the Prevention of Cruelty to Animals since he assumed charge. The working force of paid agents has increased from ten to sixteen and the total number of paid employees from twenty one to fifty-one. Dr. Rowley has been particularly active in securing additional humane legislation in his state. The law to protect horses in stables from the danger of fire is the first of its kind ever enacted. He has also secured a law by which the right is given agents of the Massachusetts society to be present at all places where animals are held for slaughter, are slaughtered or are received or delivered for transportation. Probably Dr. Rowley has done more than any other individual in this country towards creating a public opinion in favor of humane methods of slaughtering cattle, swine, and sheep.

The Jack London Club, which he founded in 1918, has enrolled more than 175,000 members who are pledged to use their influence against the use of trained animals on the stage.

The missionary work of the American Humane Education Society has been expanded by Dr. Rowley by placing ten additional workers, some of whom only give part time, in the field. The foreign work has been enlarged by the appointment of additional foreign representatives, and the publication and gratuitous distribution of large quantities of humane literature printed in several different languages.

Dr. Rowley has been able to exert a valuable influence along the lines of animal protection and broader aspects of humane education through his able articles in *Our Dumb Animals*. He has also prepared a large number of leaflets and pamphlets, especially on the humane slaughter of animals, that have received a wide circulation, and he is the author of " The Humane Idea," one of the best concise histories that have been written on the humane movement. His public addresses on the broader humanity have charmed many audiences all over the United States with the beauty and grace of their delivery, and have won his hearers to a better under-

DR. FRANCIS H. ROWLEY
*President, Massachusetts Society for the Prevention
of Cruelty to Animals since 1910*

standing of their duty towards the brute creation.

Dr. Rowley was born in Hilton, N. Y., July 25, 1854, the son of John Rowley, M.D., and Mary Jane (Smith) Rowley. He was educated in the public schools and the University of Rochester, receiving his degree of A.B. from the latter institution in 1875. The next three years were spent in study for the ministry at Rochester Theological Seminary, from which he received the degree of B.D. In 1897 he was honored by his alma mater with the honorary degree of Doctor of Divinity. In 1878 he married Ida A. Babcock, of Rochester, N. Y. They have one daughter and three sons.

Some two years before the death of Mr. Angell he appointed Mr. Guy Richardson as the secretary of The Massachusetts Society for the Prevention of Cruelty to Animals and The American Humane Education Society, recognizing his superior qualifications for this important work. For a number of years Mr. Richardson had been closely associated with the editorial and business desks of large newspapers which gave him a wealth of valuable experience in efficiently handling the editorship of *Our Dumb Animals,* to which he succeeded on the death of Mr. Angell in 1909. Under his direction the magazine has been brought to a high standard of the publisher's art. As the secretary of the two societies, he has an extensive correspondence with humanitarians in this country and abroad, which has enabled him to keep in very close touch with the development of the anticruelty movement. Many have come to know him personally by meeting him at the annual gatherings of The American Humane Association, where he usually has a large exhibit of the literature published by his societies. He has contributed some excellent papers before these meetings on various phases of humane education and has taken a prominent part in the development of Humane Sunday and Be Kind to Animals Week, as a national observance.

Dr. William O. Stillman
*President, The American Humane Association
1905 to 1924*

CHAPTER V

DR. WILLIAM O. STILLMAN AND THE AMERICAN HUMANE ASSOCIATION

THE name of William O. Stillman will be always associated, in the minds of humanitarians, with the first great national development of the anticruelty cause in the United States. In 1905 he was first elected President of The American Humane Association. He found the work weak, demoralized and ineffective. When he assumed office the Association had few members, very inadequate income and small influence. It had no regular office, no paid employees and did little more than hold annual conventions, at which addresses were made and discussions took place. The Association published an annual report, which, unfortunately, had little influence in moulding public sentiment. Its existence yielded small results.

As years passed, under President Stillman's management, all this was changed for the better. A strong national organization was gradually built up, with many of the most distinguished names in the United States included among its list of honorary officers. Representative humanitarians are found on its Board of Directors. It became an honor to be connected with its work and to be included in its membership. Large offices were secured and filled with well trained employees. An official monthly magazine was established. This goes everywhere and is widely quoted. It prints tons of humane literature, which finds a circulation throughout the United States and in many other countries. The work has become truly nationalized and has received much international recognition. In 1914, President Stillman was elected the President of the First International Federation of Societies for Animal Protection, in London, England, and has received honorary certificates and diplomas from many lands. Mainly through his efforts, The American Humane Association has become the effective national champion of the humane cause in the United States. It has been found ever ready to fight humane battles and to stand unflinchingly for humane principles. When Dr. Stillman first assumed the presidency of The American Humane Association there were 280 anticruelty societies in the United States. The last humane census shows that there are 565 active societies.

Bergh, Angell, Gerry and a host of other humane leaders, began their labors when legislation in behalf of children and animals was practically non-existent. The cause was not popular. Their efforts were subjected to more or less opposition; popular approval did not come at once. Sometimes the masses ruled them out because their sports were stopped and the press was slow to recognize the justice and ethics for which they contended. But time produced changes. The unselfish labor of the pioneers first aroused interest; then commanded respect and finally won admiration. It became good form to be referred to as a humanitarian. Those high in public life came to recognize the importance of stimulating organizations that took the Golden Rule as their motto and extended its application so as to include even the animal world.

Able local humane leaders, however, were slowly developed. Here and there a man or woman was found who recognized the need of the anticruelty movement. Some enthusiasts attempted to build their work on mere sentiment. The results accomplished were ephemeral. Others applied practical business methods to ameliorate the hard lot of the unfortunate and achieved success. Many labored hard for a time but became discouraged at the unresponsiveness of their communities and gave up the fight. Those that persevered gained the victory, and their accomplishments serve as memorials to their intensive struggles. Most of the successful workers regarded their own field of labor as so vast that they gave little aid to those who toiled in neighboring cities. National leaders were few and far apart.

The precarious existence of The American Humane Association, which was founded in 1877, was at times discouraging to its friends. Much had been undertaken, but there was needed able leadership to coordinate its activities and to unify humanitarians. In 1905 matters reached a crisis. The President who had been elected was appointed to a diplomatic post in Russia, leaving the presidency vacant. Where was his successor to be found. Who would he be? It was at this juncture that the Directors of this Association turned to a popular humanitarian at Albany, New York, who, some years before, had taken a struggling local humane organization and built it into one of the most flourishing anticruelty societies in the country. They prevailed upon him to assume the presidency. To-day, the name of Dr. William O. Stillman and his work are known wherever humane societies exist through the world.

William Olin Stillman was born September 9, 1856, in Normansville, a small town on the outskirts of Albany, N. Y., the only child of Rev. Stephen Lewis Stillman and Lucretia Miller Stillman. His father was a well-known Methodist clergyman who traced his ancestors back through early Colonial history to a prosperous English family. His mother's people were of Holland Dutch stock and served the Colonies during the Revolutionary War. At the age of twelve, he lost his father and removed with his mother to Albany. As a boy, he was a great lover of books and acquired a library of more than 1,200 volumes before his twelfth birthday. He delighted in the study of comparative religions and history, and was quite the despair of his mother's pastor, who could only meet his arguments for religious liberalism by sending him home when the disputes became too intense. The spirit of toleration which he then developed has always been one of his marked traits and has enabled him to view great fundamental principles of ethics in their broadest application to man and the sub-human species.

In 1878 he received the degrees of M. D. and A. M. from Union College, and, though the youngest member of his class, he was graduated with the highest honors. The next five years were spent as a physician in a sanitarium at Saratoga Springs. He married Miss Frances M. Rice, of Boston, Mass., in 1880. Nearly all of 1883 and 1884 were spent by Dr. Stillman and his wife in Europe, where he studied medicine in London, Paris, Berlin, and Vienna. On his return to America he took up the practice of medicine in Albany, N. Y., rapidly achieving success and prominence in his profession.

For many years he taught the history of medicine in the medical department of Union University. In spite of an ever growing practice, he found time to write on medical matters. During the Bicentennial of the Granting of the Charter of Albany as an incorporated city, he was appointed chairman of the committee on historical exhibits. The loan exhibition gathered through his efforts was valued at three-quarters of a million dollars. The inspiration of this exhibit led to his founding of the Albany Historical Society, which now has a splendid home of its own, and possesses a very valuable collection of historical antiques and modern paintings. His own collection of Indian relics is highly prized by the society. A few years later he correctly located the battle of Bennington, which led ultimately to his being elected President of the New York State Historical Association.

A society for the prevention of cruelty to children was organized in Albany County, New York, in 1887, and incorporated the following year. In 1889 the society took the name of The Mohawk and Hudson River Humane Society. An Albany County Society for the Prevention of Cruelty to Animals was organized in 1892. Two years later the two societies were consolidated under the title of the former. This was

the first time in the State of New York that this
title was used for the combined work of child
and animal protection. For two or three years
Dr. Stillman had been an inactive member of
the Children's Society, but was dissatisfied that
so meritorious an institution should be doing so
small a work. Without solicitation on his part,
he was elected President of The Mohawk and
Hudson River Humane Society in 1892.

As soon as he could shape a program, the
society began to make a stir in Albany and
nearby Troy, where it was then functioning.
Dr. Stillman became a zealous advocate of
humane ideals and also a fearless prosecutor of
the cruelist. Often he investigated the cases
himself and appeared in court to represent the
society. When he found his agents were spend-
ing more time in the office than in the discharge
of their duties, he released them and tried others.
By means of this selective process and careful
training he developed some first-class humane
agents, but the thought was impressed upon him
that at some time a training school must be
created which could supply anticruelty organizations with efficient and satisfactory officers.

Gradually, demands were made upon his organization to handle cases in adjoining counties,
as the effectiveness of the society became known.
To meet this, he caused branches to be organized
until there are now twelve counties and twelve

cities included in the jurisdiction of The Mohawk and Hudson River Humane Society. Each county has its own individual Board of Directors, but is amenable to the central board. The year before Dr. Stillman took charge, less than 300 children and animals were cared for. This gradually increased until 10,000 children and 20,000 animals were being cared for by his society annually. The income increased from $700 to over $40,000 yearly. The working force grew from one employee to over thirty.

The need of children's shelters and headquarters in Albany and Troy caused Dr. Stillman to launch building campaigns in both cities, which were successful. A splendid stone structure was erected in Troy through his initiative. It cost complete nearly $75,000, and has been copied in other cities. The resourcefulness of Dr. Stillman was illustrated by an incident in obtaining the Albany building, which had been a large, well-built hospital. The hospital had moved to a suburban site and the property had come into the hands of a wealthy real estate operator who intended to raze the structure and erect ten modern flat houses on the site. Plans were drawn and work was ready to start; even some of the prospective houses were leased, before Dr. Stillman realized how well adapted the building was to the purpose of the society. Without money for a building fund, he visited the owner and told him of his desire to have the society own the building as a shelter for unfortunate children. President Stillman said, "Wouldn't you rather the building were converted into an institution where years after you are gone its walls will be sheltering helpless, maltreated children, than to make it yield you a money income that will disappear with your lifetime? Allow the society to acquire it and you will build a monument that cannot be effaced." "Come back in two days," was the laconic reply. The answer which was given two days later was satisfactory, and after a whirlwind campaign, funds were secured by which the society acquired a magnificent, great building, covering 125 feet on two streets, that houses its principal offices, furnishes a large shelter for children; also the roomy headquarters of The American Humane Association and the American Red Star Animal Relief. It further provides a large amount of profitable renting space. When the building was dedicated it was entirely paid for. It is in the very heart of Albany, and increasing in value yearly.

Within the last few years a large shelter and office building was purchased for the branch in Schenectady. Midway between Troy and Albany, the society owns a valuable rest farm for horses, on which it has erected a model shelter building for small animals. The society here cares for lost and stray dogs and unwanted cats in five cities, and also looks after dog license enforcement. The property of the society is very valuable, the Albany shelter having originally cost over $200,000, and the society has a very substantial and steadily growing endowment fund. The organization is one of the strongest in the United States. Its policies and operations are recognized as models and have been widely copied.

Dr. Stillman has always been an advocate of team work. Public sentiment is shaped by mass action. He accordingly affiliated with the New York State Convention of Societies for the Prevention of Cruelty to Children and Animals. The year following his election as President of his local society, he attended The American Humane Association and International Humane Congress held in Chicago, Ill., in 1893, under the presidency of John G. Shortall. Two years later he was made a Vice-President of the Association. His paper on " Live Birds as Targets," which was read at the Washington meeting, in 1898, attracted wide attention among humanitarians throughout the country. At the Buffalo meeting, in 1901, he was placed on the Executive Committee, and in 1903 became one of the Directors. By this time his judgment was being sought on every question of importance by state and national humane leaders.

At the St. Louis meeting, in 1904, Dr. Albert W. Leffingwell was elected President of the Association, but on being appointed Consul to Warsaw, Russia, he resigned his position with the Association. Dr. Stillman had been much talked of for the place at the annual meetings, so that the Directors knew that in selecting him to fill out the balance of the term they would make no mistake. The meeting for 1905 was held in Philadelphia, where Dr. Stillman was reelected unanimously, as has been the case with convention after convention ever since.

When he assumed his duties, the Association had no office, furniture or equipment. There were no employees. Its total receipts for the year, contributed by a very limited number of people and societies, were only a few hundred dollars. Interest was at a low ebb. Men and women who should have been supporting it held aloof and criticised because it did not exhibit greater efficiency. An executive was needed who could break down overconservatism; could command the confidence of the groups of humanitarians who represented different shades of opinion; could work out a program that would weld the societies together into one strong working body, for common good. It needed someone who could stimulate public interest by written and spoken messages, and could build up an endowment that would insure continuity of effort and provide stability. Fortunately, these qualities have been abundantly exemplified in Dr. Stillman. They account for the steady growth in size, influence and usefulness of The American Humane Association.

The present place of leadership attained by The American Humane Association was not reached in a night. There were plenty of discouragements. There was indifference from those who should have lent support; provincialism in humane affairs had to be dealt with tactfully; money had to be raised to meet growing demands for literature and office employees; the future must be safeguarded by raising a suitable endowment; legislation had to be sought and means provided for its introduction in State Legislatures and, at times, in Congress. Humane education needed to be extended by the passage of compulsory humane education laws, and the creation and distribution of quantities of humane literature. The story of the Association's growth in these many channels would require too much space to tell in detail. Only a few of its larger achievements, during Dr. Stillman's administration, can be mentioned. Three things were declared by Dr. Stillman as essential to the best development of humane work in America. They were: (1) A humane magazine that could present the humane cause as a whole and truly be the mouthpiece of local

*Headquarters of Mohawk and Hudson River Humane Society, and since 1906
Headquarters for The American Humane Association, Albany, N. Y.*

societies. (2) The service of a humane "re-
vivalist" and organizer. (3) The creation of a
training school for humane workers.

The first office of The American Humane
Association was equipped with a typewriter
and some furniture loaned by Dr. Stillman. A
stenographer was employed, and a broadside of
letters sent out for society and individual membership. As the returns came in, humane literature, in ever-increasing volume, was asked for,
and correspondence with all parts of America
and with many foreign countries began to grow.
Additional help was employed. In 1911, Mr.
Robert H. Murray, of Halifax, was employed for
a few months to deliver humane lectures in colleges. In December, 1912, Sydney H. Coleman, who had been Manager of the Erie County
Society for the Prevention of Cruelty to Animals, Buffalo, N. Y., for two years, was permanently engaged as Field Secretary. January, 1913, saw the birth of *The National Humane Review*, with Dr. Stillman as editor.
It is now all that its founder anticipated,—
the chosen mouthpiece of the anticruelty societies of America. It goes to every state in the
Union and is read in practically every civilized
country in the world. Through its columns,
humanitarians are kept in touch with the most
significant phases of child and animal protection.

Long before our country entered the war,

Dr. Stillman began writing regarding the suffering that American horses were undergoing, when purchased and transported by the belligerents for use on the battlefields of Europe. The Royal Society for the Prevention of Cruelty to Animals, of London, England, had created a service early in the war that was proving of great aid in reducing the hardships of British army animals. The probability that the United States would be drawn into the struggle was so evident to Dr. Stillman that he proposed to the Secretary of War that The American Humane Association should provide a similar service for the American Army. On May 22, 1916, Secretary of War Baker accepted the offer and sent the following letter to Dr. Stillman:

WAR DEPARTMENT
WASHINGTON,

May 22, 1916.

Dr. WILLIAM O. STILLMAN,
President, The American Humane Association,
287 State Street,
Albany, New York.

Dear Sir:

The War Department is in receipt of your communication offering the services of your Association and its five hundred allied societies in organizing and maintaining personnel and supplies available to the Government in time of war for rendering assistance to wounded animals employed by the Army, and appreciates your offer very much.

All countries in time of war must depend to a large

degree on the voluntary assistance of its citizens, and
especially is this so in the case of the sick and wounded,
both men and animals.   Such voluntary assistance to
be of the greatest value in war, however, must be organized, trained and equipped in time of peace, as only
in this way can full coordination be maintained between the regular and volunteer forces.

The President in 1911 proclaimed the American
Red Cross to be the only volunteer society authorized
to render aid to its land and naval forces in time of
war, and that other societies desiring to render similar
assistance could only do so through the American Red
Cross.   This society is at present organizing base hospital units and other formations, some complete in both
personnel and equipment, and some composed of personnel only.   Personnel for these is secured from among
people trained by reason of civil occupation in the
duties they would be called upon to perform in time
of war, and in the event of war each unit, complete,
would be available for assignment to some prearranged
station for duty.

The function of the American Red Cross is to assist
the Government in caring for the human sick and
wounded in its armies.   The American Humane Association could very well function in a similar manner in
assisting the Government in caring for the sick and
wounded animals in its armies.

Such assistance would be very gratefully received
by the War Department, and it is suggested that you
write to Colonel J. R. Kean, Director General, Department of Military Relief, American Red Cross, Washington, D. C., who will inform you in detail as to the
proposed plans of that society.

It is believed that plans similar in tenor to those of
the Red Cross could be very advantageously adopted
by your Society for rendering organized aid to injured

9

animals in time of war, and if your Society will undertake this work, the War Department will be very glad to cooperate with you.

Very sincerely,

(Signed)   NEWTON D. BAKER,

Secretary of War.

This new and important venture was called the American Red Star Animal Relief, after an international movement formed for the relief of army animals that had been started in Switzerland, in 1914. Dr. Stillman became the Director-General of the organization in the United States. Steps were immediately taken to popularize the work and 125 branches were organized throughout the United States. Large sums were collected and a satisfactory plan for the distribution of veterinary supplies was effected. Drugs, medicines, bandages and instruments were rushed to the cantonments, during the early days of the war, at the request of the veterinarians to meet their needs until they could be obtained through the regular government channels. Eleven large motor ambulances, each capable of carrying two animals, were built in England (at the request of the American army headquarters) and given to the American Expeditionary Force by the Red Star at a cost of more than $60,000. In accepting them, General Pershing wrote: "They will be of great service and will be turned over to our Veter-

inary Corps for its exclusive use." They proved
to be a most valuable aid in caring for sick and
disabled animals and won high praise for the
Red Star from the Chief Veterinarian. Seven
other ambulances, motor or horse drawn, were
furnished army cantonments and camps in this
country. A two-wheeled horse ambulance, designed and built by the Red Star, proved so
popular that the Government constructed a
large number of them.

Many of the camps in this country covered
so much ground that the veterinarians found it
difficult if not impossible, to look after all of
the animals in their charge. The Red Star, accordingly, purchased four automobiles and ten
motorcycles, seven of which had sidecars, and
placed them in various camps for the use of
army veterinarians. They served a most useful
purpose and caused camp commanders to write
warm letters of appreciation to Red Star headquarters. In some instances supply buildings
were erected at a cantonment. A First Aid
booklet for army animals was prepared for the
Red Star, by an experienced army veterinarian,
to be distributed gratuitously among the soldiers handling army animals. It was exceedingly popular. More than 150,000 copies were
distributed among the soldiers at the request of
army officers and veterinarians. The American
Red Star Animal Relief was of great value, not

only in the relief afforded army animals but also in the impetus given to animal protection in scores of cities in the United States and its possessions. Local anticruelty societies were able to recruit many new workers among those who first had their interest aroused by aiding in the development of the Red Star operations. Permission was granted the Red Star to erect an artistic bronze tablet in the War and Navy Department Building, at Washington, D. C., commemorating the indispensable service rendered by the animals lost in the war. It was duly executed by an able artist and placed in the entrance hall of the great War Department Building of the United States, adjoining the White House, in Washington, D. C., where it was unveiled by the President's wife, Mrs. Warren G. Harding, and accepted on behalf of the Government by Major General W. A. Holbrook for permanent preservation.

At the close of the war the American Red Star Animal Relief turned its attention to the problems of animal protection that were too large for individual societies to successfully handle. For years, humanitarians had been greatly concerned with the enormous number of cattle and sheep, amounting to more than 2,000,000 annually, that died on the Western ranges from starvation, thirst and exposure. In previous years The American Humane Association had given extensive publicity to this frightful condition. Now, the Red Star again took up the task. A careful survey of conditions was made by experienced agents and a searching publicity campaign was directed against it. Thousands of leaflets were distributed among the school children of the range states and valuable methods also were suggested for the correction of the evil. Conditions have greatly improved as a result of this campaign.

The prompt dispatch of a considerable sum of money to the Director of the National Park Service by the American Red Star Animal Relief saved thousands of elk, in Yellowstone Park, from starvation during the spring of 1920. The hay that was bought to supplement the natural forage, which lay several feet under the snow, preserved a magnificent herd, the largest in America, from possible extermination. The Red Star stands ready to meet similar crises whenever they may arise.

In the spring of 1919 Mr. Albion E. Lang, for a long period a Vice-President and liberal supporter of The American Humane Association and a member of the War Council of the American Red Star Animal Relief, guaranteed $5000 annually to The American Humane Association, for a period of five years, for the employment of a humane " revivalist " and organizer. Mr. Lang delights in extending a helping hand to the better protection of animal life. His thorough familiarity with the working plans of The American Humane Association convinced him that such an organizer could best function through it. Mr. R. C. Craven, who had skilfully directed the affairs of the Toronto Humane Society and who, since the summer of 1918, had been Publicity Director of the American Red Star Animal Relief, at its headquarters, was selected for the position. It was a difficult work, but he has met its problems successfully. Thousands of miles of travel have been necessary to fill the calls that have come for the services of the revivalist from nearly every state in the Union. New societies have been organized; many old ones have been rejuvenated; large numbers of lectures have been given, and thousands who first have heard of humane work and its importance have enlisted under its banner.

Thus another of Dr. Stillman's ambitions for the movement has been realized. He regards it, however, as just a start. He believes that the funds will be provided so that not one, but a dozen, organizers may be scattered throughout the states, and that ultimately missionaries may be sent into foreign countries to carry the message of humanity, as is being done in the states.

In 1910 the First American International Humane Conference was held in Washington, D. C., under the auspices of The American Humane Association.   Representatives were present from thirty-two foreign nations or political subdivisions, and delegates were present from nearly every state.   President William H. Taft served as its first Honorary President.

Dr. Stillman also was the presiding officer at the Second American World Humane Conference, which was held in New York City on October 22-27, 1923.   Delegates were appointed from thirty nations.   There were members and delegates from many parts of the United States and Canada, as well as from Mexico and South America.   Nearly every country in Europe was represented, including Spain and Turkey. There also were representatives present from India, China and Japan.   It was the largest and most successful humane conference hitherto held and celebrated the centenary of the passage of the first anticruelty law, by a legislative body, through the efforts of Mr. Richard Martin, in the British Parliament.   There was great enthusiasm and the utmost interest was manifested.

An interesting feature of the Conference was the presentation of a gold medal to Dr. Stillman, as President of The American Humane Association.   The medal was given by the American Society for the Prevention of Cruelty to Animals.   It was composed of virgin gold, with the seal of the society presenting it on one side, and with the following inscription on the reverse:

"Awarded to Dr. William O. Stillman, President The American Humane Association, in recognition of his distinguished service to the cause of animal protection, 1923."

Another notable incident of the occasion was the presentation to President Stillman of a morocco bound book, with his initials in gold on the outside. The book contained the text of a finely illuminated inscription, on vellum, reading as follows: "The Second American World Humane Conference and the 47th Annual Meeting of The American Humane Association, in session in New York City, U. S. A., October 22-27, 1923, present this testimonial of their high appreciation of the eminent service, local, state, national and international, rendered to the cause of humaneness by Dr. William O. Stillman. As a prophet and a reformer he has hoped and loved and endured; as a humanitarian statesman, Dr. W. O. Stillman has instructed, inspired and achieved; as a friend he is true and strong and tender. That his bow may long abide in strength is the wish of a grateful constituency." The book contained, in a special pocket, a United States Treasury Bond from his many friends as a token of their appreciation and affection.

Humane Sunday and Be Kind to Animals Week observances are now very generally held. They originated through a resolution passed at the 1914 meeting of the Association held in Atlantic City. The Presbyterian Church has been induced to establish a special humane department in charge of an experienced director, and the Protestant Episcopal Church and the Baptist organization have passed resolutions endorsing the preaching of humane sermons in their churches. The Federal Council of Churches of Christ in America has also gone on record as favoring the humane movement, while other religious bodies have likewise passed similar resolutions.

As a further means of popularizing humane work the Association originated annual national humane poster and essay contests. These have been widely observed by hundreds of thousands of school children and have resulted in the first original art work ever available for anticruelty propaganda. The missionary value of these posters and essays has been very great.

Few persons, except those coming in the closest touch with Dr. Stillman, have realized at how great a sacrifice he has indefatigably conducted his local and national humane work. His professional skill quickly gave him a large clientele, sufficient to engage all of his waking hours. He enjoyed the opportunity of befriending the poor. There stretched before him a career of usefulness, strictly within his profession, that would have made him a wealthy man. It offered him the means for travel, art and literature. He loved them all passionately. His vision of community service, however, was bigger than his personal pleasure. He preferred to become a public benefactor with its resultant discouragements, its sacrifices, but likewise its attendant satisfaction of having achieved something bigger than professional glory or financial reward.

The first offices of the local and the national humane movements were given space in his own home until they could afford quarters of their own. He still maintains his personal offices at his house, to which stenographers and clerks go daily. His daily humane schedule gradually came to take up more and more of his time until his professional work was necessarily contracted. His humane work day starts at eight-thirty in the morning and continues uninterruptedly until twelve or one. In the afternoon he likewise finds time for humane conferences. In the evening he spends from eight until ten o'clock, frequently until midnight, working out humane plans, going over his correspondence and solving the problems presented by local societies. So exacting and heavy has this become that he rarely takes a holiday and never enjoys a full twenty-four hours on his beautiful country place along the Hudson, that fairly teems with animal life and which he loves and admires. His dogs, his horses and his poultry, of many kinds, are all objects of his interest and concern.

Few men are more closely in touch with the

world events or the latest in books, but his familiarity with them is gleaned by employing a secretary to read to him at meal times. No moment is lost. He has always at hand reading matter to refresh and stimulate him to greater activity if perchance a breathing spell occurs in his daily routine.

He has many hobbies which contribute to his enjoyment and relaxation. Reference has been made to his historical research. He has acquired a wonderful library, which includes many rare volumes. His studies of painting, architecture and sculpture are extensive. He has wonderful collections of curios drawn from all parts of the world. Until within the past few years he delighted in his driving horses, which are now pensioned on his farm. He is an ardent motorist, but will not permit himself to take extended trips because of office duties.

From the founding of The Convention of Societies for the Prevention of Cruelty in New York State, he has been active in its counsels, serving it for nineteen years as a Vice-President, and now as its President. In 1914 he was elected President of the International Federation of Societies for Animal Protection at a meeting held in London. For nine years he was Chairman of the New York State Humane Education Committee. He has been active in securing state humane legislation and has frequently gone to Washington in behalf of Fed-

eral laws. Among other honors and activities
are: Physician to Open Door Mission and
Hospital for Incurables, 1887-8; Babies' Nursery and Lathrop Memorial, 1888-92; Home for
Christian Workers since 1892, etc.; lecturer on
history of medicine, Albany Medical College,
1896-1914; awarded gold medal at St. Louis
Exposition, 1904, for philanthropic services;
silver medal, Ohio Humane Society; gold medal,
San Francisco Society for Prevention of Cruelty to Animals; honorary member of Finland,
two Italian, Argentina and Cologne (Germany) societies for prevention of cruelty to animals, Federated Humane Societies of Pennsylvania, Michigan State Humane Association:
Honorary Vice-President of Audubon Society
of State of New York, President New York
State Historical Society, member of American
Peace Society, New York Peace Society, American Association for the Advancement of Science, American Academy of Political and
Social Science, American Geological Society,
etc.

The contributions he has made to the humane
movement are sufficient to entitle him to a big
place among the worthy reformers, but he has
found other avenues of service. In 1905 he
founded a short term training course for women
who desire to be nurses and give scientific care
to the sick at prices within the reach of the poor.
Large classes are sent into service each year to

carry on their good Samaritan labor. He anticipates the development of a " Poor Man's Hospital," before he must cease his activities, that will place modern hospital conveniences within the reach of all who need them.

Those who have heard him speak or have read any of his numerous writings are familiar with his polished and terse style. His knowledge is exact and covers a wide range of subjects. His word pictures have won many converts to the humane cause, an ever growing circle of readers who recognize his strength of purpose and soul greatness. He is an admirable presiding officer and his fund of ready wit has saved many tense situations and much personal bitterness.

Probably no living humanitarian has a larger acquaintance or warmer personal friends, in this country and abroad, than Dr. Stillman. Men and women are drawn under his influence by his magnetic personality. He commands confidence by his sane judgment and well executed programs. The genial smile, the apt phrase, the appreciative word are always ready to lift up the discouraged and spur others on to greater achievements.

Among those who have been closely associated with Dr. Stillman, none has served longer or more efficiently than Nathaniel J. Walker. He entered the employ of The Mohawk & Hudson River Humane Society as a young man. Dr.

Stillman recognized his admirable qualifications and made him Superintendent of The Mohawk & Hudson River Humane Society. He has been connected with the society nearly thirty years, at first as a clerk, then as Superintendent and later as Secretary. He finally became General Manager. He also became associated with his chief as Secretary and Legislative Agent of The Convention of Societies for the Prevention of Cruelty in New York State, and has been Secretary of The American Humane Association since 1908. To these varied positions, Mr. Walker has brought abilities of a very high order. He is an excellent speaker, and has addressed acceptably many assemblies. He has also written valuable papers on humane topics, which have been presented at national Conventions and have been printed and widely distributed, owing to the demand created by their intrinsic merit. As an executive officer he has few equals, and directs many subordinates. Although not an attorney, for years he has been trying cases before the courts, and has won a great percentage of convictions while seeking redress for his humane clients. This has been done by his knowledge of law, and by his skill, tact and persuasiveness. He has shown admirable judgment in handling the many cases brought before him, and has exhibited a humane sympathy and interest which made his work greatly respected and admired wherever it has been known.

CHAPTER VI

MEN PROMINENT AS LOCAL HUMANE LEADERS IN THE UNITED STATES

CONDITIONS in America were ripe for humane expansion in 1866. It simply needed the galvanic action of Henry Bergh, in New York, to electrify a score of cities. Men and women of influence, in their respective communities, had been stirred deeply by the daily cruelties enacted upon their streets but had felt their helplessness in dealing with them. The story of The American Society for the Prevention of Cruelty to Animals was told in newspapers widely scattered. Sometimes it was treated as a huge comedy; at other times sympathetically. The results were the same. A solution was offered for a long standing curse. The path had been blazed. It now needed but the perpetration of some glaring case of brutality or a little encouragement from the right source, to insure the organization of a society in large cities everywhere.

In the course of more than fifty years there have arisen hundreds of workers whose unstinted

labor and self-sacrificing spirit entitle them to a
large place in the affection of humanitarians.
Were an attempt made only to list these devoted
and pioneer souls, it would require a volume.
Some day such a compilation undoubtedly will
be made. In this chapter only a few names can
be included. They have been selected not necessarily because they served more than others, but
because their contribution marked an era or
some significant advance in humanitarian progress.

Philadelphia was the first city after New
York to take action in behalf of animal protection. Mr. M. Richards Mucklé, then manager
of the *Philadelphia Ledger,* had viewed with
heavy heart the acts of cruelty that took place
daily in the street in front of his office window.
An account of Mr. Bergh's work had come to
his attention and he determined that a similar
program was required in Philadelphia. On
April 28th, 1866, he caused a notice to be inserted
in the *Bulletin,* in which he asked those interested in the formation of such a society to com-
municate with him. A few of Mr. Mucklé's
personal friends became aroused and a meeting
was called for May 6, 1867, to consider preliminary plans. Mr. Bergh was invited to attend,
but the press of local affairs prevented his acceptance. He did write, however, most encour-
agingly, and closed his letter by saying: "I

COLONEL M. RICHARDS MUCKLE
*President, Pennsylvania Society for the Prevention
of Cruelty to Animals, 1896 to 1915*

would not exchange places with the President of the United States if by so doing I were hereafter to be barred from further service in this most beneficent cause." The meeting was held and plans made for a subsequent one.

It is most interesting that Mrs. Caroline Earle White, of revered memory, should have been working on a similar project during 1866 and 1867. From the time of her marriage to Richard White, a prominent Philadelphia lawyer, who came from Ireland and had told her of the Royal Society for the Prevention of Cruelty to Animals, she had hoped for such a society in America. In the summer of 1866 she had called on Henry Bergh, in New York, and at his suggestion had returned home to enlist support for such a society. Both she and Mr. White had circulated petitions and secured many signatures of prominent people advocating the formation of a society for the prevention of cruelty to animals. She had not seen Mr. Muckle's call and only heard of his activities through correspondence with Mr. Bergh. On learning what he was doing she called upon him and offered her assistance, which was gratefully received.

On June 21, 1867, another meeting was called, at which the Pennsylvania Society for the Prevention of Cruelty to Animals was instituted. The following Spring, April 4, 1868, the Pennsylvania legislature granted it a charter with state-wide jurisdiction, which had been drawn by Mr. Mucklé. Dr. Wilson C. Swan was elected President and served one year. Several very prominent Philadelphians were elected to the Board of Managers, including Mr. White. Neither Mrs. White nor any other woman was given an elective place in the management, for at that time women were not commonly accorded such distinction. Mr. Morris S. Waln, who became the society's second President, gave the new movement a great impetus by a gift of $6000. During the Presidency of Mr. Waln, he suggested that a "Women's Branch" be instituted. This was done April 14, 1869, with Mrs. White as its President. Her work will be traced in another chapter.

From the first Col. Mucklé took a leading part in the development and guidance of the society, but refused repeatedly to accept the presidency, preferring to work in the ranks. The position was held for several years by prominent gentlemen, including Robert W. Ryerss, who became the society's chief benefactor and whose wife left funds for the development of the notable Ryerss Infirmary for Dumb Animals. Mr. Ryerss was President from 1885 until his death in 1896. At that time the friends of Col. Mucklé persuaded him to accept the position of President. During the balance of his life he devoted himself very largely to the affairs of the society.

Scarcely a day passed but found him at his desk, looking after its detail operations and wisely planning for its future when he must entrust the work to others.

Col. M. Richards Mucklé was born in Philadelphia, September 10, 1825, and died there in 1915. After securing an education in the public schools he entered the office of the *Public Ledger*. By dint of hard work and application, he was advanced to the rank of general manager, a position he held for many years. During the Mexican war he was offered a second lieutenancy. In 1853 he was appointed on the staff of the Governor of Pennsylvania, with the title of Colonel. His ability as a public speaker caused him to be in demand and brought him prominently before the people. He was among the first to suggest and advocate the Centennial Exposition which was held in Philadelphia, in 1876. Col. Mucklé's faculty for organizing was of great service to the Pennsylvania Society for the Prevention of Cruelty to Animals from its very first days. Before the charter was even granted, he caused an agent to be employed to begin constructive work. He insisted on a sound financial policy which has proven a bulwark of strength during the entire history of the society. Probably no society for animal protection in America has its future more securely guaranteed than the one he served for so long a period.

All through a long and busy life Col. Mucklé found opportunity to assist many worthy philanthropies, but of them all he cherished and loved best the society which cared for dumb beasts.

Fortunately for the welfare of the society, Mr. J. Gibson McIlvain, Jr., was selected, in 1916, to succeed him. Since 1906 Mr. McIlvain had been a manager of the society and thus absorbed the viewpoint of Col. Mucklé and came to know the many different sides to the movement. More than that, he was a man of large business interests whose presence on the board of control of any philanthropic work would add prestige to its standing in the city and state. His interest in the society has never waned.

More than thirty years ago Frank B. Rutherford secured a position with the Pennsylvania Society for the Prevention of Cruelty to Animals as a complaint clerk. Later he was advanced to the position of Operative Manager, which was created for him, and William T. Phillips was advanced to the place of Secretary. The administrative duties of this large organization rest mainly in the hands of Mr. Rutherford. He has proven himself ingenious in discovering improved methods for handling anticruelty work. He was the first to introduce the electric horse ambulance and many other appliances now generally accepted as essential for successful humane management. Under his direction the society has grown to large proportions. In 1917, it dedicated a beautiful building at 922-924 North Broad street, Philadelphia, which is in every way well suited to house a highly developed anticruelty society. It owns two electric driven and a gasoline motor horse ambulance and operates a number of runabouts for agents to patrol the streets. Since the society's inception in 1867 to January 1, 1921, its agents handled 1,192,203 cases of cruelty and 17,826 prosecutions. Mr. Rutherford has done much to advance anticruelty work through the state. He helped to organize the Federated Humane Societies of Pennsylvania, of which he was at one time the President. He has originated much humane legislation, including the " old horse bill " which regulates the sale of worn-out horses and the law governing the working hours of the horse. Mr. Rutherford is an officer of The American Humane Association and takes an active part in its annual meetings. He was also a member of the Executive Committee of the American Red Star Animal Relief and has been Associate Editor of *The National Humane Review* from its first issue.

The Auxiliary to the Pennsylvania Society for the Prevention of Cruelty to Animals is composed of a group of able women who conduct some of the special work now commonly handled by animal protective societies. It maintains a large number of drinking stations for horses, and two motor water carts that provide water to the horses in the heavy teaming districts, where other watering facilities are not available. It also has a gravel car, from which tons of gravel are sprinkled on the streets when pavements are slippery. The Auxiliary also holds an annual Horse Tag Day and a large work horse parade. The supervision of the work of the Auxiliary is in the hands of Mr. John F. Cozens, who has been engaged in humane work for more than twenty-five years. He originated the watering station idea and perfected the horse watering car. He was also the founder of National Horse Day.

The records of the Illinois Humane Society state that on March 25, 1869, the Illinois Society for the Prevention of Cruelty to Animals secured its charter from the state of Illinois. Mr. Edwin Lee Brown was elected the first President of the society and held that office from 1869 to 1873. The outrageous conditions prevailing in the stock yards had been the outstanding evil that impressed the six founders with the need for such a society. Until 1877 it largely confined itself to fighting the cruelty which it found there. In the autobiography of George T. Angell he tells of a visit made to Chicago, in the fall of 1870, at the request of Hon. John C. Dore, who later was the President of the Illinois

Society from 1873 to 1875. Mr. Angell remained six months in Chicago at a heavy expense to himself, but before he left he succeeded in arousing considerable public interest by articles in the papers and through a mass meeting. Mr. Edwin Lee Brown was a man of constructive ability and a warm friend of animal protection. He became widely known to humanitarians a few years later when he was elected first President of The American Humane Association. The transportation of live stock was at that time a source of great abuse. Mr. Brown had seen it in all of its worst phases as the shipments came into Chicago. He was accordingly looked to for advice and help to solve the problems involved. He was President of the Association from 1877 to 1884, and again from 1888 to 1890.

In 1877 Mr. John G. Shortall was elected President of the Illinois society. He had been associated with the group of men who organized the society, although he was not listed as one of the founders, in the article " Reminiscences " appearing in the *Humane Advocate* for May, 1906. He was, however, one of its original directors, and it is around his work as President, from 1877 to 1906, that much of its most important history is written. The work that was being done in New York by the society for the prevention of cruelty to children attracted his atten-

tion in 1877, and led him to extend the scope of
his own organization to include children as well
as animals. The title of the society was then
changed to the Illinois Humane Society. It was
the first society in the world to do a joint work
for children and animals and the first to use the
name humane. Since then it has been applied
practically to all societies performing a dual
work. The first legislation for children in Illinois was secured the same year.

Mr. Shortall was a nationally known figure
in humane circles. He was a lawyer with a most
genial and sympathetic nature, who was born in
Dublin, Ireland, September 30, 1837, and
brought to America in his early youth. As a
man of twenty he came to Chicago, where he
studied law and was admitted to the bar. Shortly
before the great fire of 1871, he became the
owner of extensive real estate abstracts, which
later acquired exceptional value when the public
records were burned. He died July 23, 1908. It
was a call signed and sent out by him that
brought into being The American Humane Association. Throughout his life he devoted a good
deal of attention to the progress and development of the Association and was its President in
1884 and later from 1893 to 1898. He had the
satisfaction of seeing his local society expand by
developing branches in various cities in the state
of Illinois. The society was among the earliest

to use the horse ambulance for the removal of sick and disabled animals. He was the leading spirit and one of the donors in acquiring the fine headquarters building at 1145 South Wabash avenue, Chicago.

Band of Mercy work and the erection of horse drinking fountains were early made prominent features of the society's activities. In 1893 the society, in conjunction with The American Humane Association, conducted a humane exhibit at the World's Fair. The same year The American Humane Association held its annual meeting in Chicago and joined in an International Congress of Humane Workers. It was presided over by Mr. Shortall.

In 1900 Mr. Shortall gave up his public activities and was succeeded in the presidency of the Illinois Society by his son, John L. Shortall, who, with the exception of one year, continued in office until 1918. He enlarged the work started by his distinguished father. His most conspicuous service was the inauguration in 1907 of a course of lectures on humane work, held in the society's building. The lectures for drivers were especially popular and were continued for a number of years. He continues most active in the affairs of the society as a member of the Executive Committee and its Vice-President. He is likewise closely connected with The American Humane Association, of which he was Direc-

tor and Vice-President for a long period. Mr.
Shortall is a successful lawyer and associated
with many important business interests in his
home city.

The administrative officer of the Illinois
Society, since 1906, has been George A. H.
Scott. His legal training has been of great assistance in conducting the affairs of the society.
Both child and animal protection have been energetically handled by Mr. Scott, who has made
a most thorough study of the transportation of
live poultry and is an authority on the subject.
He has been active in securing humane legislation in Illinois. At various times he has prepared important papers for the annual meetings
of The American Humane Association. His
summary of humane legislation which appeared
in *The National Humane Review* was the most
complete that has been made. He is a faithful
attendant at annual meetings of the Association
and is a director. He is a humanitarian of great
ability and devotion, always to be relied on.

The Humane Advocate was launched in 1905
as the official magazine of The Illinois Humane
Society. It was published monthly until quite
recently under the editorship of Miss Ruth
Ewing. It now appears at irregular periods.
In order to establish closer relations between
the humanitarians of the state, the society took
the lead in calling a State Humane Convention

in 1908.   It has been of great use to the cause.
Mr. Solomon Sturges is now President of the
society.

The San Francisco Society for the Prevention of Cruelty to Animals, of San Francisco,
Cal., is said to owe its origin to the squealing
of a pig.   Back in the Spring of 1868, a pig
escaped from a drove on the San Francisco
waterfront.   Its shrill squealing, caused by the
brutal way in which two *vaqueros* attempted to
recapture it, brought Mr. J. S. Hutchinson into
the street to stop the outrage.   He had heard of
the work being done by Henry Bergh across the
continent and he resolved that San Francisco
should have a society that could prevent such
scenes as he had just witnessed.   The organization was soon perfected and Mr. Hutchinson became the first treasurer of the society, a position
he filled until his death in 1919.   His son has been
elected to succeed him.

In 1883 Mr. John Partridge took out a membership in the San Francisco Society for the
Prevention of Cruelty to Animals.   He was not
content to be simply a passive member.   His attention was called to the dog pound, where the
most cruel methods were employed in handling
the dogs that were brought there for disposal.
He resolved that the work should be transferred
to the society and began a long fight to this end,
which ultimately resulted in success.   In recog-

nition of his services, he was elected President of the society in 1903. The same zeal that marked his first struggle to secure justice to animals has followed his long official record. He gives close attention to the detail work of the organization, and may view its praiseworthy career with no little personal pride. Mr. Partridge is a director of The American Humane Association. His advice and suggestions have been of great use to the national movement. He was one of the founders and the first President of the California State Humane Association, formed in 1909, to free the state from the curse of fake anti-cruelty organizations and also aid in securing desirable humane legislation. The splendid quarters of the society, its large and small animal ambulances, and its sound financial position are due in a large measure to Mr. Partridge's exceptional executive ability.

In all that the San Francisco Society for the Prevention of Cruelty to Animals has done since 1895, Mr. Matthew McCurrie, its Secretary, has taken an important part. As an administrative officer of an animal protective society he has few equals. He knows the work in its minutest details and has developed many progressive ideas which have been passed on to sister societies. When the society began its excellent monthly magazine *Our Animals,* in 1911, he became its editor. Year by year the literary and artistic

qualities of this publication have improved until
it ranks with the best in its class. At the Pan-
ama-Pacific Exposition, held in San Francisco in
1915, his society had its own building, in which
was housed a valuable exhibit of humane material and devices. When the State Humane Association was formed, he became its Secretary, and
ever since has been one of its leading figures.
Frequently he has travelled long distances to
be present at the annual meetings of The American Humane Association, where he is always a
prominent figure. His practical knowledge, his
genial nature, and his typical good sense are
qualities that have earned for him a host of
friends in all parts of the United States.

The second Society for the Prevention of
Cruelty to Children was organized in Rochester,
N. Y., October 6, 1875, only a few months after
the New York Society had begun its epoch-
making work. It has had a long and honorable
history. During the past decade it has made
unusual progress and owns a well equipped headquarters building and children's shelter. No little credit for its success is due its President for
many years, Hon. George A. Carnahan, and its
efficient Superintendent, Mr. Richard S. Red-
fern, who recently resigned, and has been succeeded by Whitcomb H. Allen.

Reference has been made elsewhere to the organization of societies for the prevention of cru-

elty to children through the stir made in distant
cities by agents of the New York society in fer-
reting out evidence to complete some of its cases.
The California Society for the Prevention of
Cruelty to Children, of San Francisco, was one
of these. It was accomplished, through the sensational rescue from a circus of little Harry Mc-
Cabe, an eight year old acrobat, by Col. Charles
Sonntag, at the request of the New York society. He was so moved by the usefulness of such
an organization that he called together some of
his friends and brought about the incorporation
of the California Society for the Prevention of
Cruelty to Children, in August, 1876. Col.
Sonntag served the society as President for sixteen years, resigning in favor of Mr. E. W. Newhall, whose father and uncle were among the in-
corporators. Mr. Newhall became associated
with the society in the early eighties, as did his
brother George A., who had been treasurer for
more than thirty years and was for a time its
President. Mr. E. W. Newhall assumed the
position of President in 1903 and continued in
office until a short time before his death in 1915.
He was an active worker in the California State
Humane Association and aided materially in the
organization and development of the children's
court in his state. For a number of years he was
active in the affairs of The American Humane
Association. Mr. Newhall's place in the Cali-

fornia Society has been filled by his son, Almer
M. Newhall. As far as can be learned no other
anticruelty society in the United States has the
unique distinction of having had three genera-
tions of one family sufficiently interested to assume the burdens involved in its active management. The practical work has been for years
under the able management of Secretary M. J.
White, who is familiar with every phase of child
protection work. Mr. White is well known in
California for his progressive methods. He has
been an Associate Editor of *The National Humane Review* since its initial number, and is untiring in his devotion to his society.

Child protection was started in Brooklyn in
1880, through the efforts of Mr. Henry R. Jones,
who was elected first President of the Brooklyn
Society for the Prevention of Cruelty to Children. For thirty-three years he devoted nearly all
of his time to the development of the society.
When failing health caused him to resign he was
made President Emeritus. He died in 1916.
The active force in charge of the very large work
of this society for several years was Arthur W.
Towne, who became its Superintendent in 1913.
Mr. Towne broadened the scope of the society's
activities, and was very active in its work. He
was succeeded by Mr. Chas. H. Warner, in 1922,
who has long been associated with child protection work in New York State. He has the back-

ground of several years of social work and a legal training which helps him to meet the problems of his society with broad vision. From 1914 to 1919 he was Secretary of the Convention of Societies for the Prevention of Cruelty in New York State.

The Rhode Island Society for the Prevention of Cruelty to Children, of Providence, is among the oldest of its kind. Since 1905 it has been under the management of its able Secretary, Thomas B. Maymon. Unusual conditions have compelled the society to assume many functions not ordinarily handled by such organizations. Mr. Maymon has the true vision of the child protectionist and, by the quality of its work, has placed his society among the foremost social agencies of his state.

The late John A. Blaffer, of New Orleans, La., was one of the charter members of the Louisiana Society for the Prevention of Cruelty to Children, in 1892. He was one of its most active supporters and helped to make it the largest society of its kind in the South. In 1902 he was elected President of the society and served until 1913, when failing health caused him to resign. He took a deep interest in The American Humane Association and was one of its directors. Mr. Tudor B. Carre is now President of the society and has helped to carry it successfully through trying experiences.

Mrs. Caroline Earle White

*Founder and President of the Women's Pennsylvania
Society for the Prevention of Cruelty to
Animals, 1869 to 1916*

Hon. Robert J. Wilkin, Judge of the Brooklyn Children's Court, once said that the first time he saw the sign of the New York Society for the Prevention of Cruelty to Children he laughed at the apparent futility of such an organization, little realizing that within a brief time he was to become intimately associated with it. When the Brooklyn Society for the Prevention of Cruelty to Children was organized he was appointed its Superintendent and retained that position until he was elevated to the Bench of the Children's Court in 1903. Judge Wilkin has made an enviable reputation for his court. He understands children and realizes the underlying causes that bring them before him. Probably few are better known than he among those engaged in child protection work. He has framed many of the laws of New York that apply to children. His papers on various angles of child protection have been highly valued at the annual meetings of The American Humane Association, of which he was long a director. From the origin of the Convention of Societies for the Prevention of Cruelty in New York he has been most active in its work. He was its Secretary from 1890 to 1903, when he was elected President to replace Hon. Elbridge T. Gerry, who had resigned that position. In 1913 Judge Wilkin resigned and was made Chairman of the Executive Committee. He is a humanitarian from conviction, whose labor has been of great value in the development of humane sentiment in behalf of children.

The Connecticut Humane Society, of Hartford, Conn., is a product of the missionary labors of George T. Angell. It was incorporated in 1881 and gives attention to abandoned old people, certain phases of children's problems and the prevention of cruelty to animals. From 1899 to the time of his death in 1918, Rev. Wm. DeLoss Love, Ph. D., was its President and guiding force. In 1919 the society secured the services of Mr. H. Clay Preston as General Manager. It was a wise selection. Almost immediately he began to find new avenues of usefulness for the society. The work in Hartford was increased; the old headquarters were sold to advantage and a fine new site with excellent buildings was secured. Work throughout the state is being strengthened by the development of local organizations. Few workers in the whole movement were better equipped by training and personality than Mr. Preston to develop this large field. He began his anticruelty career in Binghamton, N. Y., with a society dealing only with animal protection. Soon child protection was added to its functions. His success led to his appointment as Superintendent of the Brooklyn Society for the Prevention of Cruelty to Children, where he added new laurels for effi-

ciency and executive ability. In 1913 he resigned, and later accepted the General Manager-
ship of the Erie County Society for the Prevention of Cruelty to Animals, in Buffalo. While
he was in its employ the society erected a modern
headquarters building and hospital. From 1904
to 1914 he was Secretary of the Convention of
Societies for the Prevention of Cruelty in New
York State. He has likewise taken an active
part in national humane work and has presented
many able papers at the annual meetings of The
American Humane Association, of which he is a
director. Mr. Preston's contribution to the
humane cause is a large one.

Humane work in the state of Oregon has
broadened out of late years. The headquarters
of the Oregon Humane Society are located at
Portland, with Col. E. Hofer as President and
Mrs. F. W. Swanton as general manager. Col.
Hofer is known as a publicist in the western
coast states, and as a man of affairs, particularly
in his own state. Mrs. Swanton is thoroughly
efficient, and as the result of the intensive labors
of herself and Col. Hofer the society occupies an
enviable position in public esteem. The work is
state-wide, and it is of such value that it has been
accorded a considerable financial appropriation
by the state. One of its achievements has been
to cut down the losses of range stock due to exposure and starvation. Hon. Robert Tucker, of

Portland, Judge of the Circuit Court of Oregon, has been a loyal friend of the Oregon Humane Society. He served as President until his judicial duties prevented. The American Humane Association enjoyed his advice as one of its directors. For several years Mr. Joseph E. Rudersdorf was the manager of this society but he resigned his position to resume his connection with the Spokane Humane Society that had prospered under his management. Mr. Charles M. Farrer, President of the King County Humane Society, of Seattle, Washington, has shown great interest in the work and labored zealously in its behalf. Mr. L. V. McWhorter is another citizen of the State of Washington, connected with the Yakima County Humane Society, who has done conscientious work.

When Mr. Huntington Smith, of Boston, Mass., perfected his electric cages for the humane destruction of small animals, in 1911, he did much to lessen the suffering of small animals that must be destroyed. The cages are the result of much experimental work and have replaced the lethal chambers of many anticruelty societies. Mr. Smith was the Managing Director of the Animal Rescue League of Boston, which was founded by his wife. Before entering his present field of usefulness he was a successful publisher, and has written extensively on many subjects. Another Boston humanitarian,

MRS. MARY F. LOVELL
*Secretary, Women's Pennsylvania Society for the
Prevention of Cruelty to Animals*

who has accomplished much for the humane cause through the development of work horse parades, is Mr. Henry C. Merwin. His valuable work is referred to elsewhere.

The Rhode Island Society for the Prevention of Cruelty to Animals, of which the Hon. Addison P. Munroe is President, owes much to Mr. James N. Smith, who has been with it since 1889. He became General Agent in 1895 and was among the first to utilize the automobile for the investigation of country cases. The society has built up a large endowment fund. Col. F. E. Boothby, now deceased, was a prominent figure with the Maine State Society for the Protection of Animals, of Portland, Me. In Lowell, Mass., Mr. Charles F. Richardson is a most successful agent of the Lowell Humane Society. He has been in charge since 1898.

Among the oldest humane officers, in the point of service, is Mr. Thomas S. Carlisle, the efficient Superintendent of the Women's Pennsylvania Society for the Prevention of Cruelty to Animals, of Philadelphia. He made a number of extensive surveys for his society, and later for The American Humane Association, on the transportation of live stock. In Washington, D. C., Mr. John P. Heap has done much to rid that city of abuse to animals, and has been connected with the work for many years.

Binghamton, N. Y., has accomplished splendid things for the humane cause. The President of the Broome County Humane Society and Relief Association is Mr. Z. Bennett Phelps, who helped reorganize the society in 1900. He was also President of the state humane organization for a term. The Superintendent, Mr. S. J. Koerbel, is exceedingly active and an able worker. Practically all of the charitable work of the city is now in his hands. The society raises a budget of more than $50,000 a year.

The prosperous condition of the Rochester Humane Society for the Prevention of Cruelty to Animals, of Rochester, N. Y., was largely due to the untiring efforts of the late J. B. Y. Warner, who was long its President. He was a great advocate of humane education and developed it extensively in the public schools. He had an able lieutenant in Mr. Frederick L. Dutcher, who followed Mr. Warner as President. He was a Director of The American Humane Association and was elected to the Judicial bench. Judge Dutcher was succeeded by Dr. W. V. Ewers as President of the society. He is a sincere friend of the cause.

A number of men have accomplished much for animal protection in the South. Among these are Mr. W. F. Crall, of Norfolk, Va.; Mr. Max Myerson, of Jacksonville, Fla.; Col. George McC. Derby, of New Orleans, La., and Col. Joseph F. Burke at Atlanta, Ga. Mr. Peter P.

Gluck, of New Orleans, has been active in behalf of the Louisiana State S. P. C. A. Mr. Henry F. Lewith, of Charleston, S. C., has worked alone but has a great deal to show for his labor. He is an enthusiastic animal lover and coined the phrase " Be Kind to Animals," and conceived the idea of " Be Kind to Animals Week." He also induced the *Charleston American* to publish a very large Be Kind to Animals Week supplement, in 1919. Mr. Lewith furnished the copy for a twenty-four page edition. It was the first venture of its kind and the largest newspaper edition devoted exclusively to anticruelty work ever published. He has produced a similar number every year since and deserves great credit.

The Western Pennsylvania Humane Society, of Pittsburgh, Pa., was founded through the efforts of Mrs. Caroline Earle White, President of the Women's Pennsylvania Society for the Prevention of Cruelty to Animals, of Philadelphia. The first effort, in 1871, was only partially successful, but was followed up in a few years, and a permanent organization effected. In the beginning the society confined its attention to the protection of animals, but later enlarged its field to include children. In 1916, Mr. H. Lee Mason, Jr., was elected President, after serving for two years as its acting President. He has proved a splendid and wise executive. Under his administration the society has made wonderful strides. It recently erected a building of its own to serve as a headquarters and ambulance house. The Secretary and Superintendent is Mr. John S. Ritenour, who was for many years editor of the *Pittsburgh Dispatch*. He was one of the original organizers of the society and its first Secretary. No man in the humane field is more respected than Mr. Ritenour. Mr. J. R. Park, of Pittsburgh, has also accomplished fine work.

Ohio has had its share of prominent humanitarians. Mr. James M. Brown, as President of the Toledo Humane Society, built up a strong organization in that city. From 1899 to 1904 he was President of The American Humane Association and did important work for the national movement. His son, Mr. Walter F. Brown, succeeded him in the Presidency of the Toledo Humane Society. In 1893, Mr. Charles C. Ware became the chief agent of the society. He has been particularly alert in the prosecution of delinquent parents and was one of the organizers of the Ohio Federation of Humane Societies. He is a very able and successful officer. In recognition of his long and faithful services, his society has given him a life appointment.

Rev. William A. Robinson, D. D., is an example of a church leader who has become prominent in humane affairs. In 1907, he was elected President of the Ohio Humane Society, of Cincinnati, and has always shown deep interest. He became a director of The American Humane Association at its Indianapolis meeting in 1912. For a number of years he was ably assisted by Mr. Oscar A. Trounstine, who was Secretary and General Manager of the society until his death in 1918.

Youngstown, O., has produced Mr. Frank L. Baldwin, Secretary and Counsel of the Youngstown Humane Society. Mr. Baldwin is an attorney and has made use of his legal training to advance the interests of his society. He is now a director and the second vice-president of The American Humane Association. From Columbus, O., comes Mr. Eugene Morgan, Secretary and Attorney of the Humane Society of the City of Columbus. He is a director of The American Humane Association and most active in its behalf. Both Mr. Morgan and Mr. Baldwin have played an important part in securing humane legislation and building up the Ohio Federation of Humane Societies. The latter is President of the Federation. Other notable Ohio men are Dr. Homer S. Ainsworth of the Van Wert County Humane Society and Mr. James E. Ewers, executive officer of the Cleveland Humane Society, which is doing a very valuable work for children.

Rev. A. W. Ryan, D. D., was the President of the St. Louis County Humane Society, of

Duluth, Minn., and of the Minnesota Society for the Prevention of Cruelty. The executive officer of the latter society is Mr. Sam F. Fullerton, who is one of the most zealous workers in the field. It was due to Dr. Ryan that the eighth Provincial Synod of the Episcopal Church passed a resolution endorsing humane work. He was a director of The American Humane Association and died in October, 1922. The agent of the Duluth society is Mr. John G. Ross, one of the leading exponents of modern anticruelty methods.

Omaha is the center of a progressive humane movement. Mr. Fred S. Martin is the President of the Nebraska Humane Society. With Mr. Welcome W. Bradley, as Secretary, the society is setting new standards of excellency. It has been particularly active in promoting humane education among school children and the development of child protection. Mr. H. S. Mann is entitled to much credit for the recent great development of the Nebraska Humane Society. A bequest by the late George Joslyn of $50,000, and another by the late Dr. George L. Miller, who founded the society in 1875, have given the society the basis of a fine endowment fund. It has recently erected a splendid group of up-to-date buildings for its work.

East St. Louis, Ill., is proud of its St. Clair County Humane Society. Mr. James K.

Ewing, its Secretary, has advanced it to an enviable place in the humane world. The Humane Society of Missouri, located across the river at St. Louis, has been recently reorganized and promises to become a strong society under the leadership of its new President, Mr. Douglas W. Robert. In St. Joseph, Mo., Mr. W. A. Ziemendorff has made a good record as Superintendent of the Humane Society of St. Joseph and Buchanan County. A modern Humane Society flourishes in Tulsa, Okla., with A. M. Welch as its executive officer.

Several successful humane societies are found in Texas. Mr. John M. Adams (recently deceased), Secretary and Treasurer of the Tarrant County Humane Society, Fort Worth, Texas, has been among the best known humanitarians in his state. He did some excellent work. Dr. Thomas A. Bray is another high grade humanitarian. He is President of the El Paso Humane Society. Rev. A. W. S. Garden is intensely interested in humane work. He was located at San Antonio, but has left the state. One of the most conspicuous humanitarians in Texas is Mr. Almon A. Locke, who has devoted his life and money to advance the interests of humane work, particularly the educational part. One of the most faithful friends of anticruelty work in Iowa has been Mr. L. C. Bissell, of Dubuque, long secretary of the society in that place. He has been a hard and consistent worker for the cause. Dr. A. E. Frederick is a notable figure in humane work in Wisconsin, where he is the State Humane Officer.

Mr. E. K. Whitehead, of Denver, is the author of a fine text book for schools on humane education. He has done much, as the Secretary of the Colorado State Bureau of Child and Animal Protection, to improve range stock conditions and modify the evils of the Round-Up shows within his state. He is the author of numerous articles on humane work. In Cheyenne, Wyo., is found the Wyoming Humane Society and State Board of Child and Animal Protection, which has jurisdiction throughout the state. Mr. E. W. Burke was the efficient Commissioner in charge of its work. He did a great deal to eliminate the abuses prevalent in handling range stock. He was a loyal supporter of The American Humane Association. The state has sustained a severe loss by his recent death. He has been succeeded by Mr. W. G. Harris, who is an ardent humanitarian.

Mr. Henry A. Pershing, the volunteer Secretary of the South Bend Humane Society, of Indiana, has been active in work among school children, and a familiar figure at the annual meetings of The American Humane Association.

Mr. C. C. Carstens, for many years Secre-

ROBERT J. WILKIN

JOHN PARTRIDGE

FRANK L. BALDWIN

MATTHEW McCURRIE

EUGENE MORGAN

tary of the Massachusetts Society for the Prevention of Cruelty to Children, of Boston, is well known among social workers. He was succeeded by Mr. Theodore Lothrop, who is a conscientious and hard worker. He has written extensively on various phases of child welfare. The Erie County Children's Aid and Society for the Prevention of Cruelty to Children, of Buffalo, N. Y., owes its present prosperous condition to the excellent work of Mr. Douglas P. Falconer, its Superintendent. The scope of the work has been enlarged, a new building has been erected, and the finances of the society placed in sound condition.

The Central New York Society for the Prevention of Cruelty to Animals, with headquarters at Syracuse, has long been doing a very active and successful work in punishing violators of laws protecting animals. For many years the President was Mr. W. S. Peck, who gave close attention to the work of his society. He has been aided by the services of Mr. O. R. Casey, Superintendent, who has been a veteran in field work without a peer in his state. The head of the Children's Society in Syracuse is President Willard A. Glen, who has long occupied the position. He is assisted by Superintendent Wm. C. Mesick, a practical and well trained officer.

A record of recent humane development in

the United States would be incomplete if no mention were made of the earnest labors of men like Dr. W. G. Hollingworth, of Utica, N. Y.; Rev. Dr. Charles Scanlon, Secretary of the Presbyterian Board of Moral Welfare, of Pittsburgh, Pa.; the late Mr. J. G. Middleton, of New Orleans; Superintendent Horace K. Ferry, of Cleveland; President James P. Briggs, of Washington, D. C.; President Irving I. Goldsmith, of Saratoga Springs, N. Y.; Superintendent Preston B. Chapman, of Yonkers, N. Y.; Superintendent John F. Hyland, of the Bronx, New York City; Superintendent Robert W. Hebberd, of Jamaica, N. Y.; Superintendent W. J. Boyink, of Rochester; Dr. H. J. Streibert, of Chicago; Father George L. Murray, of Lowville, N. Y.; Executive Secretary R. F. Sellar, of St. Louis; Secretary C. M. Young, of Des Moines, Iowa; Mr. W. H. Pingree, of Jacksonville, Fla., and a host of others whose efforts have contributed in a very considerable degree to the full realization of humanitarian success.

No anticruelty society in the States has a more able and enthusiastic President than the Toronto Humane Society, of Toronto, Can., in the person of the Rt. Rev. James F. Sweeny, D. D., Lord Bishop of Toronto. He has great faith in the value of the work performed by his society in relieving suffering. This society was organized by Mr. J. J. Kelso, who is now Superintendent of the Department of Neglected and Dependent Children, a movement that grew out of the Humane Society, which devotes itself to animal protection. This society is under the capable management of Mr. John Macnab Wilson, who was for many years a vice-president of the organization. Mr. Wilson is also Secretary of the Ontario Society for the Prevention of Cruelty to Animals, which consolidates the work of numerous similar societies throughout the province. He is a capable administrator, and both organizations, under his direction, are thoroughly successful. The Toronto Society is well equipped. It has an efficient staff, and publishes *The Humane Pleader,* a monthly magazine which promises well for the future of humane effort in Canada.

One of the most earnest workers in the humane cause in Canada is Mr. R. H. Murray, Barrister, now President of the Nova Scotia Society for the Prevention of Cruelty. He has been associated with this work for many years and takes a very active interest in affording protection for the helpless clients of his society.

It is interesting to note that two great grandsons of Mr. Richard Martin, familiarly known as " Humanity " Martin, who was the author of the first bill passed by a legislative assembly to afford protection for animals, are residents of Canada. They are deeply interested in humane matters. One is Judge Archer Martin, of Victoria, British Columbia, who occupies an important position on the bench in that section of Canada. The other is Mr. Henry J. Martin, a Barrister, residing in Toronto. Both men are worthy of their great ancestor.

MRS. H. CLAY PRESTON.

MISS ALVA C. BLAFFER.

MRS. JAMES SPEYER.

MRS. HUNTINGTON SMITH.

MRS. RICHARD HARDY.

Chapter VII

AMERICAN WOMEN AND THEIR NOBLE WORK FOR HUMANITY

THE heart of American womanhood has always been sympathetic for the lot of the unfortunate. Her deep-seated instinct for right and justice has been shown in all of the great social reforms that have grown up in this country. Wherever ministration to the lot of those who suffer has been required she has responded promptly and efficiently. Every disaster, every war, has found her ready to undergo hardship and personal suffering, if need be, to bring joy and comfort to those in distress.

Until after the Civil War social convention prevented her from taking a lead in public affairs or becoming a member of boards of control of philanthropic movements, though it was frequently her generous and devoted spirit that enabled success to be attained. It is most natural, therefore, that the preliminary work in preparing the way for animal protection should have been taken by men. In all of the early societies, however, the founders have given unstinted praise to the assistance of devoted women.

As the humane movement grew and women

began to assert themselves more and take their places alongside of men in the initiation and direction of public affairs, women came to occupy a seat of equal power in anticruelty work. In many places she has taken entire control. Without her devoted and self-sacrificing labor the humane cause could never have advanced so far or so rapidly. In fact, it is safe to say that were the support of the women of America suddenly withdrawn, the large majority of societies for the prevention of cruelty to children and animals would cease to exist.

It is no easy matter to record adequately, in a few pages, the important contributions of many women to the anticruelty cause. Many of whom no record is available have worn their lives away in struggling to right wrong and check the cruelist. Others have possessed the power of leadership and have made lasting impression upon the humane cause. A few women are referred to in this chapter, but with the feeling that there are scores omitted who are equally entitled to recognition.

Brief reference has been made elsewhere in this volume to the early efforts of Mrs. Caroline Earle White to arouse Philadelphians in behalf of animal protection. Kindness to animals was an ingrained quality of Mrs. White. She once wrote in a sketch of her life[1] that as a little girl

---

[1] Four Footed Friends, Volume 11, No. 7, October, 1912.

she was passionately fond of animals and avoided certain streets near her home because, in passing over them, she nearly always witnessed scenes of animal abuse which depressed her for days afterward. Mrs. White was born September 25, 1833, of Quaker parents. Her father, Thomas Earle, was an eminent lawyer, of Philadelphia, who wrote the new constitution of Pennsylvania. Her mother was a devoted Christian woman who took an active interest in the humanitarian work of her daughter and gave the movement the benefit of her enthusiasm and encouragement up to the time of her death in 1886.

Caroline Earle married Richard P. White, a prominent Philadelphia lawyer and member of a well known Catholic Irish family, of Ireland, in 1856. Shortly afterwards she accepted the faith of her husband and became prominent in its charitable work. From him she learned of the splendid work being done in England by the Royal Society for the Prevention of Cruelty to Animals, and with his encouragement she aspired to have a similar society founded in America. The Civil War prevented any tangible movement until its close. It is not surprising, therefore, that on learning of Henry Bergh's activities, she took the first opportunity of meeting him to learn concerning his work. They met in 1866. Her subsequent part in helping to organize the

Pennsylvania Society for the Prevention of Cruelty to Animals has been told.

In 1869, Mr. S. Morris Waln, President of the Pennsylvania society, called a meeting in his home to organize the Women's Branch of the Pennsylvania Society for the Prevention of Cruelty to Animals. Thirty ladies attended, and Mrs. White was chosen President of the new organization, a position which she held until her death, September 7, 1916, at the ripe age of 83. One of the first accomplishments of the Branch was the employment of an investigating agent. The number was increased to two before the end of the first year. Mrs. Earle, mother of the President, personally canvassed the homes in Germantown, where she lived, and raised enough money to pay one agent's full salary. Humane education became a most popular feature of the society's work and led to very gratifying results. In order to properly handle any legacies that it might receive, Mr. Mucklé, of the Pennsylvania Society for the Prevention of Cruelty to Animals, suggested that the Women's Branch be separately incorporated. Accordingly, Mrs. White, accompanied by several ladies, went to Harrisburg and secured the necessary charter, which had the effect of making it an independent society. The corporate name was changed in 1897 to The Women's Pennsylvania Society for the Prevention of Cruelty to Animals.

Mrs. White was the moving and guiding hand in all of the society's activities, although she was fortunate in having the support of several able lieutenants. In 1869 she caused the society to provide a temporary pound, conducted on humane principles, and obtained the right from the city to collect the stray and homeless small animals from the streets. In 1870 the city allowed the society $2,500 to meet the expense of this work. This was the first attempt on the part of any society in the United States to handle the problem of caring for surplus or unwanted small animals, and as far as it can be ascertained the first appropriation ever made by a municipality for humane work. Sulphurous gas was employed at first for disposing of the small animals that had to be killed. A little later carbonic acid gas was substituted as being more humane. The pound work continues to be a prominent feature of this society's work, and, following its example, it has been accepted as a part of the program of a very large number of anticruelty societies throughout the country.

Mrs. White was firmly convinced of the value of humane education in the public and parochial schools and introduced humane essay contests among the children. In 1874, with the aid of Mrs. Charles Willing, Junior Humane Societies were formed among the boys. This idea grew to large proportions during Mrs. White's lifetime.

It was the first attempt of its kind in the United States and antedates the Band of Mercy movement with which these societies were ultimately merged.

The cruelties in the transportation of live stock early attracted the attention of the Women's Branch, and Mrs. White engaged actively to suppress them. The society's agents were sent all over the state to secure evidence, and several cases were bitterly fought out in the courts. When The American Humane Association turned its attention to this work, she was made chairman of a special committee to gather evidence. An agent was sent over a large area of the United States and much good was accomplished, though far less than she had hoped for. She appeared at numerous hearings in Harrisburg, and also at Washington, in behalf of legislation to curb cruelties involved.

The brutalities connected with the horse-drawn street cars of Philadelphia were a source of much distress to Mrs. White. She sought legislation to regulate the loads of the cars and the conditions of the animals, but with little success, other than the education of the public in regard to a grave abuse. The agitation subjected her to ridicule but she moved steadily on, regardless of opposition, when her course seemed clear to her.

Mrs. White was of the missionary type. It

was not enough for her to see improvements coming in her own city in behalf of animal protection. She wished to share her progress with places less fortunate, giving them the benefit of her society's experience and literature. Her agents went through Pennsylvania, encouraging and developing the formation of other societies. Points in New Jersey, Maryland and New York profited through her liberality and enthusiasm. At one time her society attempted to maintain a colored humane missionary in the South, but without satisfactory results.

Her vision of anticruelty problems made her appreciate the value of a national humane movement. She was a delegate to the first meeting of The American Humane Association in 1877, and always continued to be one of its most ardent supporters. For a number of years she served on its Board of Directors.

Mrs. White will long be remembered for her pioneer antivivisection activities, which are covered in Chapter VIII. Probably no American figure has exercised so great an influence in this direction as she. Pigeon shoots and fox hunts received her vigorous condemnation and led her to advocate laws for their prohibition. She championed bird preservation before the advent of the Audubon Society and helped to secure protection for the Atlantic shore birds. In fact, her labor covered every phase of animal protection. Her convictions were positive and never permitted a half way or compromise course. Such a character is always misunderstood and her position was often criticised in an unkind way. Frequently harsh words were used, but she bore all harsh remarks with the patience and humility that marked her noble character.

In order to extend the influence of the Women's Branch of the Pennsylvania Society for the Prevention of Cruelty to Animals and advance the cause of antivivisection, Mrs. White caused the *Journal of Zoophily* to be started in 1892. It was published as the joint organ of the Society for the Prevention of Cruelty to Animals and the American Antivivisection Society, which she had founded. She became its editor-in-chief and continued as such until her death. This aggressive humane magazine was published under the same title until 1919, when it was entirely taken over by the American Antivivisection Society and its name changed to *The Starry Cross*. It is now edited by the very capable Mr. Robert R. Logan, assisted by Mrs. Margaret M. Halvey as managing editor, a position she has held for many years.

The Women's Pennsylvania Society for the Prevention of Cruelty to Animals was among the first of the anticruelty societies to establish watering stations for horses. It was a favorite work of Mrs. White and she caused it to be widely used in Philadelphia. It was also under the direction of her society that the horse watering car was first introduced. During the last few years of her useful life the infirmities of age prevented her from taking as active a part as she desired. In spite of this, she maintained close touch with her society, wrote much for her magazine, and kept in correspondence with humanitarian friends in many fields. On her death it was found that both of her societies and The American Humane Association had received legacies to aid in perpetuating their work.

Mrs. White necessarily gave a great amount of time to make the various fields of her humanitarian labor effective. Yet she found time to make her home a beautiful sanctuary. The charitable work of her church was very near her heart and she took a prominent part in its development, and gave to it freely of her time and money. She derived great pleasure in travel and visited Europe on several occasions. She also wrote several very creditable volumes of fiction and travel. Mrs. White was a woman of marked individuality and of high moral and mental calibre. Her life was dedicated to good deeds and her life's story plays an important part in humane history. Miss Lida H. Ashbridge succeeded Mrs. White as President and is guiding the organization into new channels of usefulness. There are other women associated with the Women's Pennsylvania Society for the Prevention of Cruelty to Animals who deserve prominent mention for their humanitarian services, but space will permit reference to only a few. The work of Miss Elizabeth Morris will be referred to in the following chapter, for Miss Morris was the founder of the first shelter for small animals in America.

Mrs. Mary F. Lovell was one of Mrs. White's most loyal and devoted co-workers. For many years she has been secretary of the Women's Pennsylvania Society for the Prevention of Cruelty to Animals. Her voice and able pen have championed the cause with great vigor and effectiveness. She has appeared many times at Harrisburg before legislative committees to speak in behalf of anticruelty and antivivisection bills. Through her influence the Woman's Christian Temperance Union established its Department of Mercy and she was made its superintendent. She has written many humane leaflets, which have been distributed by tens of thousands. Her articles in the *Journal of Zoophily,* of which she has long been an Associate Editor, have been widely read and copied. She considers " Humane Education is the real antidote to war and to all other cruelty and crime." Mrs. Lovell is a director of The American Humane Association and was its secretary from 1905 to 1907. She is President of the

Montgomery County Society for the Prevention of Cruelty to Animals, at Wyncote, Pa.

Mrs. C. W. Ritchie, who recently went to her eternal reward, was a co-founder with Mrs. White of the women's animal protective society. For more than forty-five years she was its treasurer, handling its funds with great care and efficiency.

Many other Pennsylvania women have performed most meritorious humane services. Mrs. Bradbury Bedell is President of the Auxiliary to the Pennsylvania Society for the Prevention of Cruelty to Animals, which maintains watering stations for horses, a couple of water cars, a gravel car and holds an annual work horse parade. Mrs. Bedell furnished the funds for the first watering stations in Philadelphia, and was the founder of the Animal Rescue League of that city. Mrs. Charles Willing and Mrs. Robert Harford Hare did notable humane work among children; Mrs. William B. Griggs, Mrs. Elizabeth C. Easley, Mrs. F. B. Rutherford, Mrs. Fred Thurston Mason, Miss Anna P. Stevenson, Mrs. W. G. Harding, Mrs. M. M. Halvey and many others have played an important part in developing anticruelty activities.

Mrs. Lydia Ryerss left a large legacy to endow the Ryerss Infirmary for Dumb Animals. This was the first rest farm for horses in this country. The animal dispensary maintained by the Women's Pennsylvania Society for the Prevention of Cruelty to Animals is known as the Annie L. Lowry Home for Smaller Animals. It was started with funds left by another pioneer, Mrs. Annie L. Lowry, who was long associated with Mrs. White.

Humane education has always proven a favorite field among consecrated women humanitarians. The number who have made notable contributions to this branch of humane work is legion. Among the foremost in the list is Miss Sarah J. Eddy, of Bristol Ferry, R. I. It has been said of her by well informed humanitarians that " she has probably done more to advance humane education, not only in her own state but all over the world, than any one individual in the world." The number of humane leaflets which she has written and caused to be published and distributed is extremely large. Among her most notable books are those entitled " Friends and Helpers " and " Songs of Happy Life." Much organizing work has been done through her efforts. Her services have had a far-reaching effect and will continue for years to come, to guide the thought of man and child to a better understanding of their duty towards the helpless. Her benefactions have not been limited to the good of the animal world, for she has done much to ameliorate the unfortunate lot of many of the human family. She has been so

modest and retiring in her work that many have
never heard of her name, but among humanitarians it is greatly respected and widely known.
She has done an important humane education
work for Spanish-speaking people.

Another woman who has expended large
sums of her own money in publishing and circulating humane literature, both in this country
and abroad, is Miss Mary C. Yarrow, of Philadelphia. Much of it has been the product of her
own thought. Its effective, virile style has
caused it to be widely read and quoted. The
Spanish-speaking countries have made a special
appeal to her, and much of the literature she has
sent out has been printed in that language. She,
too, has avoided the light of publicity.

Miss Ruth Ewing, of Lake Forest, Ill., is
known largely through her connection with the
Illinois Humane Society, of which she is a member of the executive committee and the only
woman who has ever served the society in that
capacity. She was editor of the *Humane Advocate* while it was regularly published by the
Society. The " Book of the Beastie," of which
she is a co-author, is a valuable contribution to
children's humane literature. She was a Director of The American Humane Association and
has served it loyally. Her interest in the Illinois Humane Education law helped materially

in having the subject featured in the Chicago Public Schools.

The work of the late Miss Emma E. Page, of Olympia, Wash., was of far-reaching effect though she had very limited means and did her writing in spite of blindness and severe bodily suffering. Mrs. F. W. Swanton, of Portland, Ore., has performed excellent work as general manager of the Oregon Humane Society, particularly for pound work and for range stock salvage.

Many compulsory humane education laws owe their origin and spread to clear thinking, hard working women humanitarians. Miss Calla L. Harcourt, of Chester, Ill., with the help of Miss Ruth Ewing, secured the passage of the first law of that kind, through the Illinois legislature, in 1909. This has served as a model for similar legislation in several other states. She was made an honorary member of the Illinois Humane Society for her legislative fight in behalf of the Illinois anti-live bird trap shooting bill in 1905. Miss Harcourt was also an ardent antivivisectionist. While her humane labor has been most valuable, she once wrote that she preferred to do her own work quietly and allow others to receive the credit.

To Mrs. H. Clay Preston, of Hartford, Conn., belongs the credit of placing New York State in the ranks of those having a progressive and practical humane education law. No general ever planned his campaign with greater care than did Mrs. Preston to get the bill through the New York State legislature. Several years elapsed from the time the bill was framed until it was introduced, but she wanted to be sure of its prompt passage before launching it. It became law in 1917. Important as was this achievement, Mrs. Preston did not rest until she succeeded in having a syllabus on humaneness prepared by the state education department. She was honored by the Commissioner of Education with a place on the drafting committee. For many years she has been secretary of the New York State Humane Education Committee. Long before the teaching of humane education became compulsory she prepared and distributed thousands of " Outlines of Study " among the teachers of the state, in which appeared a complete course of humane study for each grade. This compact, yet complete, outline was one of the most valuable ever published. She also compiled and published a list of available humane books and leaflets for the use of teachers and students of humane problems. Mrs. Preston has done extensive lecture work in the schools of Buffalo and New York City and has appeared in nearly all of the Normal Schools of New York State. She is the wife of H. Clay Preston, manager of the Connecticut Humane

Society and much interested in humane education in Connecticut. In New York City, she
has been the representative of the American
Society for the Prevention of Cruelty to Animals
in her humane education work.

Mrs. S. A. Stevens, founder of the Maine
State Humane Education Society, of Portland,
Maine, was the sponsor of the humane education
law in her state. Mrs. Stevens has since become
Mrs. Rudolph M. Gilbert. In Alabama, Mrs.
W. N. Wood, the efficient President of the Bir-
mingham Humane Society, with the help of other
noble women, succeeded in placing a similar law
on the statute books of Alabama.

Among New England humanitarians, Mrs.
George T. Angell, wife of the famous Boston humane educator, is much revered. The load of many
years prevents her from being as active as she
would like, but nevertheless she keeps well informed on the progress of humane work. Mr.
Angell gave her the credit for much that he was
able to accomplish. Her warm, sympathetic
nature gave him courage to continue his work in
spite of great opposition. Mrs. M. Jennie Kendall, of Nashua, N. H., developed a strong humane organization with state jurisdiction. Mrs.
Jennie Powers, of Keene, N. H., the Misses
Elizabeth Almy Gatter and Georgia Gatter of
Connecticut are dynamos of humane energy and
have furthered the cause in their states.

MISS ELIZABETH MORRIS

MRS. JEANNETTE RYDER

MISS STELLA T. HATCH

MRS. R. FLEMING BOWDEN

MRS. F.W. SWANTON

MRS. EDITH L. DUSTIN

The splendid accomplishments of Mrs. Anna Harris Smith, President and founder of the Boston Animal Rescue League, and Mrs. Franklin Couch, of Dalton, Mass., the founder of the Berkshire Animal Rescue League, will receive notice in another chapter. Mrs. Smith is the editor of *Our Four-Footed Friends,* a splendid monthly magazine published by her League, and she has written some of the best stories for children that have been published. Miss Elizabeth W. Olney, the Corresponding Secretary of the Rhode Island Humane Education Society, of Providence, and Mrs. May L. Hall, Secretary of the Humane Press Bureau of the American Humane Education Society, are helping to popularize humane ideals.

Reference will also be made later to the extensive work of Mrs. James Speyer, President of the New York Women's League for Animals, and Mrs. Diana Belais, the Founder and President of the New York Antivivisection Society.

The popularity enjoyed by Mrs. Minnie Maddern Fiske, the actress, has made her work in opposition to trapping, range stock evils and other cruelties, most valuable. She has aided many local societies, and whenever possible plans to give humane addresses to groups of prominent women in the various cities in which she appears. Mrs. Fiske's devotion to the humane

cause has accomplished great good because of
her intense sincerity.

There are few readers of New York papers
but have seen at one time or another open letters appealing for the welfare of animals written over the signature of " G. E." Humanitarians know this to be none other than the noble
Miss Georgiana Kendall, whose life has been a
benediction to thousands of persons and animals.
She is Vice-President of The American Humane
Association and a director of the American Humane Education Society. Miss Kendall and her
sisters give generously to the work of these and
other humanitarian organizations. Too much
cannot be said in favor of the splendid humane
work done by this fine humanitarian and her sisters.

Those who have studied the " Manual of
Moral and Humane Education," by Mrs. Fiora
Helm Krause, recognize in her an able and efficient writer and worker. Her text book is
among the best on this topic. The widely read
books of Miss Marshall Saunders have given her
a high place in the humanitarian field. She is a
prolific writer, whose books always appeal to the
best in the minds of her readers. " Beautiful
Joe " is probably the best known of her long
and ever growing list of books. Over one million copies have been printed and sold. Another
popular authoress, whose death was keenly felt

in humane circles, was Sarah K. Bolton. She was a true humanitarian, who uncompromisingly opposed cruelty in every form.

Few writers had a wider effect upon the masses in this country than Mrs. Ella Wheeler Wilcox. She was a great animal lover and wrote many beautiful poems, appealing for their care and protection. She became " the voice of the voiceless." So many and so valuable were these contributions that she was known as the " poet laureate of humanity." During the war she wrote for the Red Star and acted as its representative in England shortly before her death. She has been greatly missed.

The development of the American Red Star Animal Relief brought to light many who had never before taken an active part in humane work. One of the outstanding figures in this regard was Mrs. Anita Baldwin, of Los Angeles. She served as Chairman of the Los Angeles Branch of the Red Star and raised large sums for its use. Her services won for her the honorary title of Colonel of a regiment located at Camp Fremont. When the war was over, she was elected President of the Los Angeles Society for the Prevention of Cruelty to Animals. She has since retired. Mrs. Baldwin is genuinely fond of animals.

Mrs. Lawrence Gronlund, of Oakland, Cal., Chairman of the Humane Education Committee of the State Humane Association of California, and Mrs. Alice Park, of Palo Alto, have been great humane missionaries. As an agent of the American Humane Education Society, the latter has maintained a Humane Press Bureau from which a vast amount of valuable material has reached the newspapers throughout the country. Mrs. Park has always taken a prominent part in the Peace Movement.

Ohio has had its share of prominent humanitarian women. Mrs. Herbert Gill presides with much influencce and ability over the Humane Society of the City of Columbus. Miss Anna M. Woodward, who began her humane education work with the Rochester Humane Society, of Rochester, N. Y., is rendering important service as Secretary of the Society for the Prevention of Cruelty to Children and Animals, of Youngstown, Ohio. She is usually present at the annual meetings of The American Humane Association. In Cleveland, Miss Stella T. Hatch and Mrs. V. A. E. Dustin, co-founders of the Cleveland Animal Protective League, have built up an important humane institution under great difficulties. They also have done yeoman service in working for humane legislation. In Cincinnati, the Ohio Humane Society is under the active direction of Mrs. Theodore Workum.

Miss Alva C. Blaffer is the only daughter of

the late John A. Blaffer, a charter member of the Louisiana Society for the Prevention of Cruelty to Children, of New Orleans. For many years prior to his death she took a great interest in her father's work and aided in developing the society's activities. She is now one of its directors. She is also a director of The American Humane Association and made a special investigation for it on the treatment of children in Mexico. Her articles in *The National Humane Review* on this subject have created widespread interest in this country. Her missionary work for the humane cause in Mexico has been remarkably valuable and she has done much for animal protection and for the formation of Bands of Mercy among Mexican boys.

Milwaukee humanitarians are proud of the work of Miss Lenore Cawker, who turned her own property into a shelter for small animals when the municipal authorities failed to provide suitable quarters for a pound. The work was carried on most effectively by her, but at great personal expense. Recently the contract for this work was given to the Wisconsin Humane Society. The great work done by Miss Harriet Bird, of Stow, Mass., who established Red Acre Farm for Horses, one of the first of the kind in the United States, is more fully mentioned elsewhere. Miss Mary B. Shearer, of Baltimore,

President of the Maryland S. P. C. A., long
has carried on a large and successful society, as
has Mrs. Abner Larned, of Detroit, President
of the Animal Welfare Association of that city.
Among the most famous humane missionaries
which this country has produced has been Mrs.
Jeannette Ryder, of Havana, Cuba. Almost
single-handed she opposed the bullfight and
other cruelties in that great city. Her success
has been remarkable.

Humane work in Florida has been kept alive
through the efforts of Mrs. Jennie Weller and
Mrs. R. Fleming Bowden, President of the
Jacksonville Humane Society, who have labored
hard and successfully. Mrs. William B. Dixon,
President of the Woman's Auxiliary of the Kentucky Humane Society, now deceased, was particularly active in humane education. Child and
animal protection are looked after in Wilson, N.
C., by Mrs. George W. Stanton. In Augusta,
Ga., Dr. Sophia Davis has likewise done com-
mendable work. In Wilmington, Del., Mrs.
S. S. Deemer, now deceased, accomplished much
good for the welfare of children as President of
the Delaware Society for the Prevention of
Cruelty to Children.

Mrs. Richard Hardy became a national
figure among humanitarians through her work
for the Red Star. The Branch, which she organized in Chattanooga, Tenn., was among the

first to be formed. It raised a considerable sum of money for the national work and developed a training course in Chattanooga for those desiring to enter the army veterinary corps. For more than a year Mrs. Hardy was in charge of the New York office of the Red Star, giving her services gratuitously. Mrs. Hardy is well known in her own state for her successful work as President of the Chattanooga Humane Educational Society. She has been able to accomplish much through the public shools, where the children have been writing humane essays and drawing humane posters for several years. Mrs. Hardy is a director of The American Humane Association. She is a woman of marked ability and a great humane leader in her state, where she has done valuable work for humane education.

Among the genuine friends of the cause in the United States none has been more devoted or more deeply interested than Mrs. John J. Caulfield, of Grand Rapids, Mich. Her winter home is in Pasadena, Cal. In summer, Mr. and Mrs. Caulfield are apt to travel. The latter has written notable magazine articles on humane subjects, particularly on conditions in foreign countries. Her interest has been most practical and helpful. She gave a considerable sum of money to The American Humane Association as a memorial to her mother, the late Mrs. John E. Peck.

Among the outstanding humanitarians of the Middle West is Mrs. George Joslyn, who is an important member of the Nebraska Humane Society, of Omaha. Mrs. Joslyn has generously aided in the erection of large and important offices and buildings for the society in Omaha. There never have been developed more genuine and sincere humanitarians than Miss H. H. Jacobs and her sister, Miss Sarah Jacobs, of Kansas City, Kansas. In season and out of season, they have labored to relieve animals and have fought for their assistance with undaunted courage and marvelous ability. They deserve great credit. In the field of foreign work, particularly in South America, Mrs. O. F. Frederick, of Reading, Pa., has labored most earnestly. In Hawaii, Mrs. W. W. Thayer, President of the Hawaiian Humane Society, has done much good, as has also Mrs. Marie von Piontkowski, President of the Philippine Society for the Prevention of Cruelty to Animals. In Alaska, Mrs. Beatrice Gasser has performed excellent humane missionary work.

Buffalo, N. Y., had an organized branch of the American Society for the Prevention of Cruelty to Animals early in 1868. Among its foremost workers was Mrs. Lilly Lord Tifft. Miss

Margaret F. Rochester is the Secretary of the prosperous Erie County Society for the Prevention of Cruelty to Animals, which succeeded the first organization. She introduced the humane essay contest in the public schools, where it has been an important feature since 1894. Many other women prominent in the social life of Buffalo are active in the affairs of this society.

Among the names of those active in humane work who should not be forgotten are Mrs. Wilson Groshans, of Aurora, Ill.; Miss Bertha Shin, of Milwaukee; Mrs. Dotha Lantz, President of the Indianapolis Humane Society; Mrs. Nora Gause, the indefatigable humanitarian of Kokomo, Ind.; Miss Dora Kitto, of Vancouver, B. C.; Mrs. A. R. Benson, of Regina, Sask.; Miss Carolyn Verhoeff, President of the Kentucky Animal Rescue League, of Louisville; Mrs. Zula Valentine, of Muncie, Ind.; Mrs. Madeline K. Vandegrift, of Philadelphia; Mrs. W. W. Tryon, long of Philadelphia; and the zealous Mrs. Jennie Nichols, of Tacoma. Mrs. George E. Greene, of Dayton, is another deeply interested humanitarian, as are also the Conant sisters, of Van Wert, Ohio.

Scores of other women might be mentioned, as thoroughly deserving of recognition, who have earnestly furthered the humane cause. Their courage, their resourcefulness, their persistency, are winning battles every day for their helpless and speechless friends. Their work may appear at times to be unappreciated and barren of lasting results, but they are educating their communities, slowly but surely, to higher standards in the care and protection afforded unfortunate children and animals.

CHAPTER VIII

OTHER ORGANIZATIONS FOR THE PROTECTION OF ANIMALS GROWING OUT OF THE HUMANE MOVEMENT

A S animal protection grew in popularity in America, it was most natural that progressive humanitarians would find other channels than law enforcement, for the protection and relief of animals. The importance of humane education was borne in upon all the pioneers, and they took some momentous steps to reach the public with their message of kindness to every living creature. Shelters were created for the housing and humane destruction of small animals. It was but a step from this to rest farms for horses where animals might be pensioned by their owners or where the poor man might send his overworked animal for a brief rest at a nominal or no expense. All of these, and other activities in behalf of animals, were developed as offshoots of anticruelty societies.

THE ANTIVIVISECTION MOVEMENT

Alleged brutal and needless experimentation upon animals early attracted the attention of

American humanitarians.   Bergh, Angell, and
Mrs. White were all outspoken opponents of all
forms of vivisection.   The attempt by Philadelphia surgeons in 1871 to secure dogs for experimental use from the animal shelter that had just
been established by the Women's Branch of the
Pennsylvania Society for the Prevention of
Cruelty to Animals (later the Women's Pennsylvania Society for the Prevention of Cruelty
to Animals), thoroughly aroused Mrs. White
and undoubtedly hastened the founding of the
American Antivivisection Society.   The society
absolutely refused to comply with the request,
and was sustained in its action by the city authorities.

In the course of several visits to England,
Mrs. White had developed a warm friendship
for Miss Frances Power Cobbe, who was the
first to organize a society to oppose vivisection in
Great Britain.   She also met other antivivisec-
tionists and became greatly impressed with their
attitude.   Miss Cobbe finally persuaded Mrs.
White to organize a similar society in the United
States.   On her return home, she consulted with
her intimate friend and co-worker, Miss Adele
Biddle, daughter of a prominent Philadelphia
bank president, and they called together seven
or eight other interested women and organized
the American Antivivisection Society.   A charter was then secured from the state legislature.

Considerable difficulty was experienced in finding a gentleman who would act as President, but this was finally accomplished. Miss Biddle was elected recording secretary and Mrs. White one of the Vice-Presidents. Later Miss Biddle became secretary and Mrs. White, corresponding secretary, positions they held during the remainder of their lives.

This initial meeting was held February 23, 1883, and marks the first concerted effort in America to regulate vivisection, for such was the original purpose of the American Antivivisection Society. A few years later its purpose was altered and thereafter it fought for nothing less than its total abolishment. The movement at first was regarded by physicians more in the nature of a joke, but as bills calling for regulation began to appear in the state legislature, the medical opposition became extremely bitter and so effective that it was impossible to secure any restrictive legislation. On one occasion Mrs. White and Mrs. Mary F. Lovell, who became a most ardent champion of the antivivisection cause, were obliged to face the leading physicians of Pennsylvania in a losing fight before a big legislative hearing at Harrisburg. At times it seemed to Mrs. White and her helpers that the cause stood still, but converts were being secured and the way prepared for the formation of other societies imbued with the same purpose in other parts of the country. In 1892 the Society started the *Journal of Zoophily,* in conjunction with the Women's Pennsylvania Society for the Prevention of Cruelty to Animals. It was devoted largely to antivivisection propaganda and is now owned and published exclusively by the American Antivivisection Society.

Several prominent newspapers and magazines unexpectedly joined the Society in its struggle, giving a considerable impetus to the movement. A number of prominent physicians also came out openly in support of its program. Probably no physician gave it more encouragement than Dr. Albert Leffingwell, who contributed many magazine articles and his well-known book entitled " An Ethical Problem," to its literature before he died. Dr Leffingwell was born in 1845 and died in 1919. He was prominent in his profession and, at one time, directed the well-known Dansville Sanitarium. In 1905, he served as President of The American Humane Association until given a diplomatic post in Russia.

Some few years before the death of Mrs. White, Mr. Robert R. Logan, of Philadelphia, became President of the Society, and in that capacity continues to further its work. Mrs. M. M. Halvey is now its Secretary. Through its office at 3243 Chestnut street, the Society sends out a large amount of literature and publishes the *Starry Cross,* formerly the *Journal of Zoophily.* In Washington, D. C., the Rev. C. Ernest Smith is President of the Washington Humane Society and of the National Society for the Humane Regulation of Vivisection. He is a convincing speaker, expressing himself with remarkable clarity, and both societies are flourishing under his direction.

There are now several strong societies for the regulation or the prohibition of Vivisection. The New England Antivivisection Society has been very active in Boston. In 1911, Mr. E. H. Clement, who for years was editor of the *Boston Transcript,* became its President, a position he held until his death in 1919. In 1911 he became President of the Interstate Conference for the Investigation of Vivisection, composed of 26 antivivisection societies. An international conference was held in Washington, in 1913, under his direction. This society publishes the monthly magazine *Living Tissue.*

The New York Antivivisection Society is presided over by Mrs. Diana Belais, a talented speaker and writer. She publishes *The Open Door.* Mrs. Clinton Pinckney Farrell and Mrs. Maude R. Ingersoll Probasco, daughter of the late Robert Ingersoll, are President and Corresponding Secretary, respectively, of the Vivisection Investigation League, Inc., of New York City. They are most active and able students of this question and work incessantly to educate public sentiment against vivisectional cruelties.

ANIMAL RESCUE LEAGUES

The Animal Rescue League has represented a distinct department of animal protection, since 1874, when Miss Elizabeth Morris, of Philadelphia, established quarters where unwanted, homeless and injured cats and dogs could be humanely housed and destroyed. This was the first animal shelter in Europe or America. The work might even be traced back to 1858, when Miss Morris and Miss Annie Waln began their self-appointed task of picking up stray and unwanted cats and dogs and chloroforming all they were unable to place in suitable homes.

The animal shelter at first received aid from the Women's Pennsylvania Society for the Prevention of Cruelty to Animals, but in time it seemed desirable to incorporate it as a separate organization. This was done in 1888 under the name of the Morris Refuge Association for Homeless and Suffering Animals. The work of the Refuge grew very rapidly. Large numbers of animals have received care in its substantial buildings in a single year.

The Refuge had so many valuable features that it became the inspiration for similar organizations in France and England. Humanita-

H. CLAY PRESTON

N. J. WALKER

GEORGE A. H. SCOTT

FRANK B. RUTHERFORD

GUY RICHARDSON

rians in America adapted the idea to suit local
conditions in other cities.   The Ellen Gifford
Home, in Boston, was the first one to be established outside of Philadelphia.   In 1899, Mrs.
Huntington Smith founded the Animal Rescue
League of Boston.   So rapidly and efficiently
did she develop this organization that it came to
be the one after which a large number of other
leagues were subsequently formed.   Mrs. Smith
developed a special genius for this class of work
and raised and expended large sums of money to
promote the efficiency of her League.   The buildings have been recently remodeled and the efficiency of the League greatly increased.   In
addition to the above, the Animal Rescue
League purchased a large farm for the care of
large animals and to serve as a Rest Home.
Another feature of this really great and remarkable work was the creation of an animal
cemetery which has been very largely patron-
ized by Bostonians.   It is a model in every respect.   According to the most recent statistics
there are now thirty-six organizations in this
country devoted exclusively to animal rescue
work.   Animal rescue leagues and societies for
the prevention of cruelty to animals occupy different fields, although the latter societies may
include relief work.   The plan laid down by the
Morris Refuge has been largely adopted by the
organizations patterned after it; first, the estab-

14

lishing and maintaining of homes in which animals may be temporarily or permanently boarded by their owners; secondly, the equipping of hospitals for the treatment of sick or injured animals, and kindred work; thirdly, the providing of refuges or agencies for homeless or suffering animals where they may be received for a time, and where unwanted and undesirable animals may be humanely destroyed.

No city is thoroughly equipped to handle humane work for animals unless it has a refuge or shelter in connection with the regular S. P. C. A., or one incorporated as a distinct organization. The animal refuge movement is plainly a relief-giving one and leaves the necessary work of prosecuting offenders, for cruelty to animals on the streets, to the S. P. C. A. organizations. The public is taught through a systematic campaign, by means of circulars and the press, where injured and unwanted animals can be disposed of. In this way thousands of animals are annually removed and painlessly destroyed, which would otherwise suffer from starvation and become a serious menace to public health. At the same time the shelter affords an opportunity for many to secure valued pets, a privilege appreciated by hundreds who could not otherwise secure them.

Women have been the leaders in the development of the animal rescue league movement.

Such well known names as those of Mrs. James
Speyer, of New York City; Miss Stella T.
Hatch and Mrs. V. A. E. Dustin, of Cleveland;
Mrs. Abner E. Larned, of Detroit; Mrs. Franklin Couch, of Dalton, Mass.; Dr. Mary E. Bates,
of Denver, Colo.; Mrs. J. Norman Jackson,
Miss A. M. Brown and Mrs. T. F. Halvey, of
Philadelphia, are all associated with successful
animal rescue leagues. A well equipped league
is operated in Pittsburgh under the able direction of its secretary, Mr. J. Ralph Park. Of
course it should be very distinctly borne in mind
that many of the regular societies for the prevention of cruelty to animals operate animal
shelters.

ANIMAL HOSPITALS

The animal hospital is among the newer
phases of anticruelty work. Mr. Henry C.
Merwin, President of the Boston Work-Horse
Relief Association and the founder of the Ash-
ton Lawrence Animal Hospital, in Boston, has
stated their purpose so well that the following is
quoted from his pen: "There are many benefits
arising from the hospital. Sick and lame horses
suffer terribly from want of proper care. The
owner is too poor to employ a veterinarian, or
he employs an incompetent one; there is no sling
to save him from standing on diseased legs or
feet; there is no soaking tub for his feet or legs;

there is no hot water to relieve him from pain or inflammation. It happens very frequently that a horse is so injured in one hind foot or leg that he stands on three legs for days, sometimes for weeks, being afraid to lie down. What is the result? The sound leg breaks down, too, under the double burden, and the poor creature is in torment until death relieves him. A sling would prevent this misery.

" A free hospital need not be a big affair. It might be simply a box stall in a livery stable, permanently hired for the purpose. Every humane society should maintain something of the kind, a refuge for dogs and cats, and at least one stall in a public or private stable for an occasional horse who needs treatment, or food, or rest."

The American Society for the Prevention of Cruelty to Animals, of New York City, was the first to erect a large building especially designed for animal hospital purposes. It was completed in 1914 at a cost of $200,000. The hospital is complete in every detail. It has stalls for sick animals connected by overhead trolley with the operating room, which is equipped with the finest operating table and surgical instruments. A special section is devoted to the cases of small animals. Everything is kept spotlessly clean and sanitary. A resident veterinarian is employed to care for the cases as they come to the hospital.

The New York Women's League for Animals also built a modern hospital in New York City, where many cases have been handled. The hospital was the outgrowth of a successful animal clinic maintained for several years previously by the League. It is admirable in many respects. The Angell Memorial Animal Hospital, in Boston, is operated by the Massachusetts Society for the Prevention of Cruelty to Animals. It contains every modern device for treating sick or injured large or small animals. This building affords a practical and at the same time a beautiful way of commemorating the work of Mr. Angell. Societies engaged in animal protection in Philadelphia, Buffalo, and Pittsburgh have equipped their new headquarters buildings with some hospital facilities. Free animal clinics are a part of the work of the Animal Rescue League of Boston, the Anti-Cruelty Society of Chicago, the Cleveland Animal Protective League and societies for the prevention of cruelty to animals in San Francisco and Los Angeles, and the Women's Pennsylvania Society for the Prevention of Cruelty to Animals, in Philadelphia.

Work Horse Parades

The Work Horse Parade idea originated many years ago in England. Annual parades are held in a number of leading English cities, including Liverpool and London. In the latter city, a cart horse parade and a van (light horse) parade, are held on different dates. We do not know of any work horse parades on the continent of Europe. They are, however, annual affairs in Toronto, Halifax and Melbourne, which are located in English colonies. The first parade in this country took place in Boston, on May 30, 1903, under the direction of Mr. Henry C. Merwin, who was first to introduce the idea in this country. This was followed a few years later by a parade in New York City under the direction of the New York Work Horse Parade Association. Philadelphia was the next city to take up the work, under the direction of the Pennsylvania Work-Horse Parade Association. The parades in Boston, New York and Philadelphia are well established annual events. They are also held with more or less regularity in the following cities: Baltimore, Chicago, Buffalo, New Orleans, Cincinnati, Columbus, Springfield, Cleveland and Youngstown, Ohio; Milwaukee, Minneapolis, Louisville; Grand Rapids, Muskegon and Manistee, Michigan; Seattle, Tacoma; San Francisco, Chico, Oakland and Los Angeles, in California; Burlington and Des Moines, in Iowa; Dallas, Texas; Ithaca, New York; New Haven and Hartford, Connecticut; Houlton, Maine; Hamline, Minnesota; Fall River, Waltham and Lynn, Massachusetts;

Hanover and Nashua, New Hampshire; Portland, Oregon, and other cities.

In England the cart and the van horse parades are designed primarily for rich men and corporations. The parades in America avoid this as far as possible, especially by introducing a class for old horses, which has been a great success. In the Boston parade an " old horse " is regarded as one that has worked for ten years or more for one owner and is still in active service. The " Old Horse Class " always has many entries, and is divided into sections according to the age of the horses. Gold and silver medals and sums of money are offered as prizes. A class for " Champion Old Horses " is also arranged for those that have won gold medals in the " Old Horse Class " in previous years. In most cases the gold medal in this class, the highest prize offered in the parade, has been taken by owners possessing only a single horse. The preference is given to old horses all through the parade. The older the horse, the higher he is graded. Particular pains have also been taken to get entries from hucksters, from barrel-rack men and from the local expressmen. The horses of these owners are the most likely to be abused.

New York City was the second place to take up the horse parade movement. It was begun in 1906 under the auspices of The New York Work Horse Parade Association, of which Mrs.

James Speyer was President, but was later taken over by the New York Women's League for Animals and continued as an annual event until the war. Philadelphia has had many successful parades. They are now held annually under the direction of the Auxiliary to the Pennsylvania Society for the Prevention of Cruelty to Animals.

Those who have had any experience with work horse parades regard them with high favor as a means of publicity and of stimulating better care of work animals by owners and drivers.

HOMES OF REST FOR HORSES

As Pennsylvania justly claims the distinction of establishing the first small animal shelter, so is it entitled to the credit of founding the first Rest Farm for Horses. In 1888, while humane work was still in its infancy, Mrs. Annie Waln Ryerss left a legacy of $70,000 to found the Ryerss' Infirmary. In June, 1889, a farm was purchased about a mile from the Bustleton station, in the city of Philadelphia, and the first institution of its kind in America was formally opened. During the years that have followed, its stalls have been crowded to capacity with tired, wornout, old horses in need of rest or veterinary treatment. The farm consists of 114 acres, with abundant pasture land. The rush of wealthy people to utilize it as a place in which to pension old family favorites soon made it necessary to reserve twenty-one of the twenty-eight stalls for strictly charity cases.

It is interesting to note that, as in the case of the small animal shelters, Boston was the second city to consider the establishment of a Rest Farm for Horses. In 1899, when Mrs. Huntington Smith founded the Animal Rescue League she included in her original scheme the development of such a farm. The feature of the work, however, was not carried out until 1907. In the meanwhile, Miss Harriet G. Bird, a practical philanthropist and humanitarian, became convinced of the desirability of such an institution and, in 1903, opened Red Acre Farm, near South Acton, " with a black horse and $8.00 in the Treasury." The start can not be described as encouraging, but those acquainted with the founder needed no prophetic insight to realize that the venture would be a success. At the close of the first summer, 14 horses had been cared for; $1,100 contributed to the work, and the original barn had been made over to accommodate 15 horses, in eight box and seven straight stalls. The work grew so fast that within three years a new barn was needed to care for the horses coming to the Farm for rest and treatment. This barn contains nine stalls.

As fast as improvements or additions have

been needed at Red Acre, means have been discovered to attain them. In 1910 the Farm found itself cramped for pasture room and increased its acreage by purchase until it now has 120 acres of land, most of which is in pasture.

As already mentioned, the original plan of the Animal Rescue League of Boston included a Rest Farm for Horses. This was created in 1907 by the purchase of 21 acres at Dedham. The Farm was appropriately called Pine Ridge, and soon became an important factor in the relief and care of wornout or decrepit animals. Its work is necessarily very similar to that of the Ryerss' Infirmary and Red Acre, already described. It avoids, as far as possible, the " pensioner " and seeks to make itself of particular value to the poor who could not afford, of their own accord, to give their horses necessary rest to build them up for service. In order that as many people as possible may be encouraged to visit Pine Ridge, a special Visitors' Day is observed each spring or summer. The public, however, is made welcome at all times except on Sunday morning.

In 1918, the Massachusetts Society for the Prevention of Cruelty to Animals was presented with a farm of 160 acres at Methuen, Mass., where a large number of animals have already received care. The San Francisco Society for the Prevention of Cruelty to Animals has re-

cently established a rest farm.   The Erie County
Society for the Prevention of Cruelty to Animals,
of Buffalo, N. Y., rented a farm for such purposes
as long as it could retain a lease of a place suitable
for the work.   Several other societies are planning
to acquire them.   This line of humane work has
so much merit that it will be most regrettable if
it is not more generally employed.

ANIMAL CEMETERIES

The practice of marking the graves of favorite pets is not new, though the development of
animal cemeteries is of comparatively recent
origin.   The Duke of Cambridge is credited
with having started the first one at Hyde Park,
London, in 1881.   It now has more than four
hundred graves.   Several other small cemeteries
are known to exist in Great Britain.   Queen
Victoria and Gladstone are among the distinguished persons who have created private cemeteries and erected markers for their favorite
animals.

A celebrated animal cemetery is located on
the Isle des Chiens, near Paris.   Since it was
opened in 1898 several hundred animals have
been buried in it.   The beautiful memorial erected
to the memory of Barry, the famous St. Bernard
of the Alps, who saved the lives of forty per-

sons and was killed by the forty-first, is located near its elaborately carved entrance.

The first two animal cemeteries of size in America were the Hartsdale Canine Cemetery and the Kanis Ruhe, both commercial ventures. The former is in Westchester County and was started in 1898. It comprises five acres of ground and has more than seven hundred interments. Kanis Ruhe is at Miller Farms, Yorktown Heights, N. Y., and has received the bodies of several hundred animals since 1906. Some very handsome marble and granite stones have been erected on the graves in these cemeteries by the owners of the animals buried there.

Mr. Frank L. Myers purchased a beautiful ten acre grove, in 1907, which he has developed into an attractive animal cemetery near Hornell, N. Y. It is free to those who wish to use it, and several hundred have availed themselves of its privileges.

The publicity which has been given to the Animal Rescue League, of Boston, has made the animal cemetery on its " Rest Farm " at Dedham, Mass., as well known as any in the United States. It is one of the finest in this country. The site is ideally chosen and has been selected by many as the last resting place of their pets. There is also a large animal cemetery at the Francisvale Home for Smaller Animals near Philadelphia.

Several other similar burial grounds have been started in the United States. It is a work well in keeping with that performed by animal protective or rescue societies and may be most advantageously undertaken in connection with Rest Farms at small expense. A few dollars will buy a plot of ground near a city large enough to take care of all demands until funds are available for larger accommodations. The number of persons patronizing them will increase as information concerning them becomes known.

BIRD PROTECTION SOCIETIES

The National Association of Audubon Societies may be taken as the typical organization of its kind in the United States. It is a national organization, admirably managed and giving a most beneficial service. Since its original formation the Audubon Society has been directly responsible for the passage of the Audubon Law in 41 states. The law protects song and insectivorous birds. Its laws prohibiting the sale of plumage have been enacted in 14 states, including those containing all the large cities. The Association has been active in securing much other legislation, both state and federal, for bird protection.

It inaugurated the system of bird reservations in this country and induced the United

States Government to create 72 of them. For many years it paid the salaries of the wardens guarding these great cities of breeding water birds. There are also about 50 Audubon reservations, which it controls and protects.

This Association annually publishes and distributes about three million colored pictures of birds and twelve million pages of literature on bird study and bird protection. It maintains a corps of active field agents and lecturers; has organized more than two million children into bird study clubs; distributes stereopticon slides, moving pictures, charts and other bird study helps.

It is maintained that some of the earliest legislation for the conservation of bird life were secured by Mrs. Caroline Earle White. The records seem to show that the first Audubon Society was organized in 1886, by Dr. George Bird Grinnell, editor of *Forest and Stream*. It died out, but was revived in 1896 by the organization of several state Societies. These were federated in 1902 and later, in 1905, were merged into the National Association of Audubon Societies. It played an important part in obtaining the ratification of the Migratory Bird Treaty with Canada.

CHAPTER IX

OTHER MOVEMENTS FOR CHILD SAVING DEVELOPED FROM ANTICRUELTY WORK

THIS has well been styled " the age of the child." From the fundamental principle of justice, with natural rights guaranteed by legal process, there has developed movement after movement designed to make child life happier and more profitable; also a more fitting preparation for citizenship in adult life. Every community has organizations affording recreational facilities or promoting the physical, mental and moral development of the young. Clubs and societies are striving to bring out the best qualities in childhood and establish a basis from which may evolve finer types of manhood and womanhood. Agencies exist to rescue the child when its well-being is jeopardized by indifferent or neglectful parents or guardians. Courts planned to deal wtih peculiar problems involving children have been created. Probationary methods have been formulated to correct misguided lives, degraded or endangered by unhappy environment, and to rehabilitate them. Schools of reform, founded on new ideals and inspired in their direction by new conceptions as to remedies for human ills, are the resort for those whose cases cannot be solved without recourse to special institutions. Judgment of the courts and of the law in cases concerning children is no longer uttered in terms of vengeance and severity. Its aim, and the aim of the thousands who have bent intellect and heart to the solution of the child problem, is the formation of true character and the development of opportunity and ability to rise above subnormal surroundings.

The germination and growth of many agencies now recognized as indispensable to the welfare of the nation's child life have given emphasis to the fact that when Henry Bergh and Elbridge T. Gerry organized the New York Society for the Prevention of Cruelty to Children they gave to the child, the world over, a new *magna charta*. The basic motive in that first society of its kind is to-day the foundation principle of hundreds of similar societies scattered throughout the world. Some still adhere solely to the original purpose and program, leaving charitable and welfare service to those desiring to specialize solely along such lines but, nevertheless, with cognate motives. Other societies for the prevention of cruelty to children have also taken on collateral work as a part of their humane program. Local conditions have, to a certain ex-

tent, governed the actual scope of the child protection society's operations. Density of population, or the reverse, has frequently been a determining factor in the creation of the policy. In Ontario, Canada, for example, protection of children has been combined with the work of children's aid societies, each and every county having its children's shelter with a local volunteer governing board, but with one general policy throughout the province centered in the government department at Toronto. This department, since its inception, has been under the direction of Mr. J. J. Kelso, to whose ability and wholehearted devotion is largely due the success of the plan.

In the state of Wyoming, and elsewhere, the Commission of Child and Animal Protection also undertakes the added service of child placing and adoption. Wisconsin has appointed a state officer to direct and develop local effort for the well-being of children and the protection of animals, linking up the different agencies dealing with children in much the same manner as is done in Ontario. In Buchanan County, Mo., a shelter for abandoned children and those eligible for adoption was found to be indispensable to the work of the child protection society. The society accordingly promoted what is known as the Sheltering Arms, a charming home for little ones in a beautiful mansion with spacious grounds, in the city of St. Joseph. The society, however, placed the Sheltering Arms under the direction of a separate Board, although every child in the home is a ward of the humane society, and no child can enter or be removed, for adoption or otherwise, except at the will of the humane society. At East St. Louis, Ill., it was found necessary to operate a day nursery for children. In numerous cases men deserted their wives and children, and the St. Clair County Humane Society, rather than break up the home, has taken care of children, enabling the mother to follow gainful occupation. Thus the family has continued to be wholly, or partially, self-supporting. In many instances family differences have been dispelled, husband and wife have been brought together again and the home rehabilitated. This would have been very difficult, frequently impossible, but for the fact that the home had been retained intact. And the motive back of it all was, and is, the well-being of the child.

In the state of Ohio the law has conferred upon child protection societies the duty of collecting from delinquent and absconding fathers weekly sums for the support of their families, the money so collected being paid over to the families without deduction of any kind. This work is most successfully carried out. Hundreds of thousands of dollars are collected annually, an enormous amount of suffering is prevented, reconciliations are frequently brought about and the dependents are in no danger of becoming public charges. Through this service, also, officials of the societies are in constant touch with the deserted families and their problems, and are able to render helpful service at the time it is needed.

It would be difficult to state definitely just what organizations are a direct outgrowth of the society for the prevention of cruelty to children. It can be stated, however, that most of those designed to improve the lot of children who have not become wards of the state—such as orphans, foundlings and those adjudged guilty of crime— have come into existence since 1875. Reference will be made to a few of those that have had and are having an important influence upon the development of American child life.

THE JUVENILE COURT AND PROBATION SYSTEM

The Juvenile Court, as an institution, is of recent origin, though its underlying principles have been recognized during many years by statutes in various states. Massachusetts passed a law in 1863 requiring the separation of children and adults charged with offenses against the law. In 1877, the Hon. Elbridge T. Gerry secured passage of a law in New York State which provided that no child under the age of sixteen

" shall be placed in any prison or place of confinement or in any vehicle in company with adults charged with or convicted of crime, except in the presence of proper officers." Michigan and Massachusetts laid the basis for juvenile probation prior to 1880, though the system was not generally followed. New York made a further advance by a law, passed in 1892 through the influence of the New York Society for the Prevention of Cruelty to Children, which allowed separate trial, special docket and separate record of cases of children under sixteen. Other states injected varying features, but in none was there a comprehensive statute embodying the working features of the juvenile court, as it is known to-day, until that passed by the Illinois Legislature, April 21, 1899.

The movement in Illinois was largely the outcome of a comprehensive study made by the Board of State Commissioners of Public Charities who recommended to Governor Tanner certain changes in the law. Among the facts which had been brought forth it was shown that in the year 1898 there were 575 children charged with offenses confined in the Cook County jail, and that in the twenty months ending November 1, 1898, there were committed to the city prison at Chicago 1,983 boys, exclusive of repeaters. The only charge in twenty-five per cent of these cases was truancy.

To Mr. R. S. Tuthill, as the first presiding officer, belongs the distinction of being the first juvenile court judge in America, while Judge Hurd is recognized as " the Father of the Juvenile Court Law."

Those engaged in service for delinquent children were quick to see in the juvenile court, as established in Chicago, a wonderful vehicle for the reformation of children and their diversion from the dangerous paths along which they had thoughtlessly started. It offered a practical means of stepping between the child guilty of some offense against the law and the punishment for its infraction without minimizing the seriousness of the act in his sight or " putting a premium on the commission of the crime."

The theory of the Juvenile Court is that a child under sixteen cannot commit a crime, but is rather regarded as a victim of circumstances. It is a court for the protection and reformation of children, and Judge Hurley expressed it tersely when he said: " The child should be treated as a child." Distinction is made between delinquent, dependent, neglected and wayward children. Separate detention rooms must be provided to prevent their association with adults who may have acquired criminal ways. Shelters belonging to societies for the prevention of cruelty to children have been largely used, in those cities where they exist, to carry out this principle.

Separate hearings are provided for children, either in open court or in chambers. Many successful judges have adopted informal and unceremonious methods in conducting these hearings in order to secure the confidence of the child and thus learn from him the full and true facts of the case. In no part of the judicial system is the expert more needed than where the cases of children are under consideration.

The Juvenile Court and the probation system are inseparably interlocked. Success depends in no small degree upon the probation officers under whose direction the child is placed for a period while his environment is being changed or improved and the cause of the delinquency is removed. In the most advanced types of the court the parents or guardians are held responsible for the offense of the child, which requires probationary oversight for them as well as for the child himself.

Without question the Juvenile Court is one of the most valuable agencies in the reformation of the delinquent child. Through its influence thousands of children have been kept out of correctional institutions that have, alas, been only too often breeding places of criminal careers. The percentage of second offenders among children placed on probation is relatively small. The reform school is now regarded as the last resort. Only when all known means have been unsuccessfully employed to give a child a normal viewpoint of his moral obligation to society is he committed.

Many improvements have been made in the organization of Juvenile Courts since the plan was first evolved in Illinois, but the underlying principles therein set forth are still regarded as sound. Scarcely a state is now without some modification of the Juvenile Court for the benefit of children whose cases call for court action. Future years will see still further improvements and even better results. The rapid growth which has attended its development, however, is only another evidence that we are literally living in the epoch of the child.

CHILD LABOR ABUSES

The development of the factory system in the United States about the middle of last century created a demand for a cheap labor supply. Many of the tasks were such as might be performed by child labor, and in conformity with the old colonial notion that an idle child was the plaything of the devil, the manufacturers and the community excused themselves for abuses which they realized were being committed. Certain industries, such as textile mills, found this labor particularly profitable and few of the older factories and mines were free of the stigma of having availed themselves of it.

Conditions were admittedly bad, but no one knew how to interfere, for there were no laws designed to regulate them. Children toiled, with the consent of their parents, who were held to have property rights in them. Children of six and seven years of age were worked on ten and twelve hour shifts. There is on record, in the Bureau of Labor, a report of 1870, which tells of child workers having cold water dashed in their faces when they fell asleep at their gruelling tasks, and of being whipped with leather straps, from which pointed tacks protruded, when they were lazy or disobedient. A fire in a Fall River plant, in 1878, burned to death a number of seven-year-old children, and led to the establishment of a rule that no boy or girl under ten years should be employed in Massachusetts factories.

Statistics on child labor were not available until 1870, when 739,164 children, between ten and fifteen years of age, were recorded as being gainfully employed in the United States. The Census of 1900 showed 1,750,158 children—nearly one out of every six children between the ages of ten and fifteen years in the United States —engaged in gainful occupations, and this did not include thousands of children under ten years of age. In 1904 only fifteen states had a fourteen-year age limit for children in factories, only eight states prohibited night work for children, night messenger service was unregulated, eleven states had no age limit or other restriction, seventeen had no school attendance laws, and twenty-seven had no educational requirements for child workers. In the southern states twenty-five per cent of the mill operators were under sixteen, compared with 7.7 per cent for the northern states. Eighteen per cent of cotton mill operators were under fourteen; more than ten thousand under twelve.

Alabama was the pioneer in the movement to abolish child labor abuses. Edgar Gardner Murphy, who organized a State Child Labor Committee, in 1903, secured the passage of a law which set the highest standard then attained by any manufacturing state in the South. It was immediately apparent that a national organization was necessary if the problem was to be solved, that child labor was in its essence a national question, and that a higher standard in one state gave undue advantages to neighboring states having lower standards. Accordingly, in 1904, a group of individuals notable among whom were Edgar Gardner Murphy, Wm. H. Baldwin, Jr., Felix Adler and Mrs. Florence Kelley, invited representative citizens from all over the country to unite in the formation of a National Child Labor Committee with headquarters in New York City. Mr. Samuel McCune Lindsay also took part in the creation of the national body. In 1907 the organization was incorporated by Act of Congress.

The principal purposes of the Committee, set forth in detail at the time it was organized, were to raise the standard of public opinion and parental responsibility with reference to the employment of children; to make public facts concerning child labor; to assist in protecting children by suitable legislation against premature or otherwise injurious employment, and thus aid in securing for them an opportunity for elementary education and physical development; to aid in the enforcement of laws relating to child labor.

Owen R. Lovejoy became general secretary in 1907 and threw himself wholeheartedly into the work of promoting reform. An examination of recent state laws shows how much was accomplished in the sixteen years following incorporation of the Committee. The summary of state laws to the close of 1922 reveals the following facts:

In all but three states the age minimum for factory work and in many other employments is at least fourteen years, seven states having a minimum of fifteen years, though exemptions are permitted in many states.

Twenty-seven states (including all the most important mining states) have sixteen as the minimum age for work in mines, four have a still higher minimum, eight have a fourteen year minimum and nine have no age minimum. Fourteen states, and the District of Columbia, have laws requiring children engaged in street trades to secure permits; ten have laws affecting boys independently engaged in street work. Every state has some kind of compulsory school attendance law; twenty-six require attendance up to the age of sixteen; two require full time schooling up to sixteen for all children; twenty-six have laws requiring attendance at continuation schools.

In 1904 there were 1,750,178 child laborers in the United States; nineteen years later the number was reduced to a little more than a million. Two attempts have been made to deal with the evil by federal legislation, but the laws of 1916 and 1919 have been declared unconstitutional. The National Child Labor Committee and other organizations are now working on an amendment to the Constitution which will give Congress the power to regulate child labor, and thus bring about the emancipation of the army of juvenile toilers.

The Big Brother Movement

The Big Brother movement, which with the Big Sister organization, is now flourishing in more than a hundred cities in this country, in Canada, and in other countries, and which in-

cludes two hundred and fifty organizations that
are carrying on this individual service for under-
privileged boys and girls, had its origin in New
York in 1904. A group of forty men, members
of the Men's Club of the Central Presbyterian
Church, listened to an appeal by Colonel Ernest
K. Coulter for individual interest in boys who
had never had a chance. He asked each man to
take an interest in just one boy who had been the
victim of evil environment, to show him there
was some one who cared, who would be a sort of
big brother to him and would be of real service.
The plea was accepted, the Big Brother Movement was formed. To-day it flourishes in countries as far distant as China and New Zealand,
and in each of the three great branches of religious faith—Protestant, Catholic and Jewish.

It was apparent to Colonel Coulter, who was
Clerk of the Court and had helped to establish
that humane tribunal, soon after the Children's
Court of New York City was organized, in 1902,
that no one judge, nor dozen judges, nor hundreds of probation officers (had they been available) could indefinitely keep in human and helpful contact with the thousands of children that
were coming into the Children's Court. Often
when a boy who gave promise of useful development came into court, facing the prospect of commitment to an institution because there was no
one to give him a chance, Colonel Coulter en-

listed the interest of individual friends. Positions were found for boys with men of good-will, who were willing to show them that there was someone who cared. Others were encouraged by individual interest to continue their schooling. Often these boys had been truants and were headed for reformatories when the Big Brother became a factor in their lives. A boy once defined a friend as "a feller who knows all about yer, but likes yer jest de same," and this was the kind of friendship that was needed when the first forty Big Brothers were enlisted. For a year the work was carried on without a line of publicity, giving time to establish the fact that the plan was sound. To-day it extends not only to children who have come in contact with the law, but in its larger phase reaches out to the preventive side. It is largely due to this, as judges of many children's courts testify, that the number of children arraigned for delinquency has decreased within recent years.

Men who had always lived in comfortable homes, who had had things fairly easy in life, were soon climbing tenement steps and learning how their little brothers really lived. No man was asked to look after more than one boy. He was urged neither to patronize nor pauperize his charge but to make it possible for the boy to progress and maintain his self-respect. Giving money without some service in return, except in direst emergency, was discouraged. Care was taken that the right men got in touch with the right boys, it being realized that contact between certain temperaments would be futile. The men not only called on the boys in their own homes but had the boys call on them. Interest in the little fellows was not confined to the Big Brother, but spread to his wife or members of his family, with favorable results. As Big Brother organizations were started among Catholics and Jews, there was the assurance that boy and man in every case professed the same faith; indeed, this has always been one of the fundamentals.

In 1909 an organization of Big Sisters was started, and in May, 1917, a Big Brother and Big Sister National Federation was formed, in Grand Rapids, Mich., with the idea of affording helpful cooperation. The Federation has held conventions annually since that time, and maintains offices at 200 Fifth avenue, New York City. At the convention in Philadelphia, in 1921, Colonel Coulter was elected Founder and Honorary Life President of the organization. George MacDonald, New York, is President, and Rowland C. Sheldon is Executive Secretary in charge of the Federation's offices.

In no more convincing terms could the Big Brother movement be described than in the words of the late President Warren G. Harding: " There is no human being, no matter how humble his position, but who in some way is an example to some one else.   *   *   *   There is nothing finer in life—and I say this with my whole heart and soul—than a kindly word or deed at the right moment.   It often saves the young man and is sometimes the turning point in his life, inspiring him with renewed courage and a fresh hold on life.   The expressed encouragement that a Big Brother or Big Sister gives the youngster frequently is all that is needed to turn a liability into an asset for the city, the state, and the nation."

THE BOY SCOUT MOVEMENT

One of the most successful efforts to combat the evils and temptations of the boy gang, with its undirected activities, has been the development of the Boy Scout movement.   Its program has been built on the theory that the best in boyhood can only be brought out by placing responsibility upon its shoulders.   To witness the events of a field day of the Boy Scouts, to see them give their demonstrations of first aid, camp craft, bridge building, fire fighting, and hear them repeat in unison the scout oath, their voices charged with enthusiasm and sincerity, as they pledge themselves " To do my duty to God and my country, and to obey the scout law; to keep myself physically strong, mentally awake, and morally straight," is to be thrilled and to realize that the national boyhood has approached a new understanding of adolescent life.

Kindred movements for girls have been organized under the name of "Girl Scouts," "Campfire Girls," and other titles, with gratifying success. The programs are planned to develop the finest qualities of womanhood by giving purpose to their play and by training them in useful and practical arts.

PLAYGROUNDS FOR CHILDREN

The Playground and Recreation Association of America was organized in 1906. Among those vitally interested in its promotion were Theodore Roosevelt, Jacob Riis, Luther H. Gulick and Henry S. Curtis. The purposes of the Association are to secure wholesome play and recreation opportunities for young and old; to help cities and small communities establish year-round recreation systems and to make spare time count for a better citizenship.

In the year of organization only forty-one cities in the United States had year-round systems of recreation for their young people. The growth of the play movement under the Association's leadership is shown by the fact that, in 1922, 505 cities had year-round or summer recreation centers under trained leadership.

HEALTH AND WELFARE OF CHILDREN

Societies for the study of child hygiene, institutes for the care of crippled and diseased children, open air schools, health clinics for prospective mothers, are so numerous as to excite no comment. They exist in various forms in most localities, some maintained on a voluntary basis, others subsidized or wholly conducted by public authorities. Most of them have national affiliations.

The American Child Health Association was formed in 1923 by merging the Child Health Organization of America, founded in 1918, and the American Child Hygiene Association which was organized in 1909. The purpose of the Child Health Organization of America was to raise the health standards of the American school child. Among the active leaders in the movement were Sally Lucas Jean, Mrs. Lucy Wood Collier, Dr. L. Emmett Holt, Mrs. Frederick Peterson and Dr. Thomas D. Wood. It proclaimed health as a positive thing, teaching what to do to achieve health rather than what not to do. Since the merging of the two organizations the joint work has been considerably developed. Under the present program it is proposed to obtain a true picture of conditions relating to child health, nationally and locally, upon which to base effective action; to work through states and communities to build up, organize and develop local and state-wide health programs; to promote a more effective service for health in existing national groups, and to bring about further public information and education. The administrative office of the Association is at 370 Seventh avenue, New York City, and Mr. Herbert Hoover is its President.

The National Child Welfare Association is rendering excellent service in directing public interest to the physical, mental and moral welfare of children. The posters, pictures and booklets for educational and campaigning purposes to promote the normal development of children, issued by this Association, are unique, clever and effective. They treat on such subjects as prenatal care; proper care of babies and children; growth of the child through play, study and work; moral and religious training and cognate topics. The Association is supported by the sale of exhibit material and literature, by contributions and membership dues. The office is located at 70 Fifth avenue, New York City.

As might be expected state bureaus of child hygiene have been developed of recent years, usually as an adjunct to the department of health. The first was established in 1912; in the succeeding eight years the number increased to thirty-four. It is natural that the exact nature and extent of the operations of such bureaus vary in the different states, and is also governed by the amount of the appropriation available for the bureau, but where adequate funds have been available excellent results have been achieved, especially in the rural sections.

In addition to the work of the state bureaus an important service is rendered by the Children's Bureau, which is an adjunct of the Department of Labor, Washington, D. C. The Children's Bureau is directed by law to investigate and report on all matters pertaining to children and child life. It investigates such questions as infant mortality, infant care, birthrate, maternity care and mortality, orphanages, juvenile courts, family desertion, dangerous occupations for children, child labor, and legislation affecting children in the several states and territories. The Bureau makes intensive studies of various aspects of child welfare, social, industrial, economic and hygienic. The results of these studies have been published in a series of bulletins and widely circulated among agencies devoted to service for the child. Miss Grace Abbott, as Chief of the Bureau, directs its operations with full regard for the importance of the task.

SCIENTIFIC STUDY OF THE CHILD

Of recent years it has become more and more recognized that a considerable proportion of the cases involving children who have come within the operations of the juvenile court, humane societies and many philanthropic organizations, require scientific study and diagnosis, if the cases are to be handled in an intelligent way. The psychiatrist is now a recognized factor in social service. Many instances of juvenile delinquency present problems which can be dealt with only on the basis of psychiatric study. Within recent years the Psychopathic Institute held in connection with the Cook County Juvenile Court of Chicago, and the Judge Baker Foundation, in Boston, with Dr. Healy and Dr. Bronner, have engaged in intensive scientific study of delinquency, and in some other large centers similar work is being undertaken. The National Committee for Mental Hygiene has done much propaganda towards more general adoption of programs of this character, and, with financial support from the Commonwealth Fund and under the supervision of Dr. V. V. Anderson, has staged demonstrations which have impressed courts and probation officials with the importance and value of the psychiatric study of delinquents.

Notable among those who have paved the way in this field in the United States may be mentioned Dr. E. R. Johnstone, Director of the Vineland Training School for Mental Defectives; Dr. H. H. Goddard, who did so much to further the use of intelligence tests in study of the feeble-minded; Dr. Walter E. Fernald, who has advanced the study of the feeble-minded along many channels; Dr. Terman, Dr. Porteus, Dr. Gessell, and many others.

In the field of delinquency many studies have been made in certain sections of the United States by different investigators. Much data has been gathered in reference to the mental condition of delinquents, as well as of other people who are objects of social service activities.

Some judges of children's courts have expressed unwillingness to dispose of " repeating " offenders unless psychiatric opinion was available. Public school systems have developed in many cities systems of special classes for the training of feeble-minded, psychopathic and other types of deviate children, and it is being increasingly recognized that admissions to such classes should be on the basis of complete examination of each case. Psychiatry and psychology are being definitely enlisted in the service of justice, education and social service. Certain medical schools are giving their senior students definite instruction on the subjects of mental deficiency, juvenile delinquency, mental hygiene programs, etc. Certain institutions for mental defectives and a few so-called reform institutions have well organized departments for the scientific study of their charges. Many hospitals for mental disease have psychological laboratories where routine psychiatric consideration of patients may be supplemented by intensive psychological studies. The Boston Psychopathic Hospital is an outstanding example of such provision, with Dr. Wells, a broadly trained psychologist, heading the work. The Whittier State School, Whittier, California; the Berkshire Industrial Farm, Canaan, N. Y.; the Maryland School for Boys, Loch Raven, Maryland; the institution at Jamesburg, N. J., and the Industrial School, Industry, N. Y., are examples of so-called reformatories for juvenile delinquents, where attempts are made to apply training and treatment on the basis of scientific study of the cases. The Berkshire Industrial Farm does intensive work in this line and attempts to utilize the various vocational lines of training as well as the rich recreational life of the place in accordance with psychiatric rules.

It is often the judgment of high-class executives in humane work that psychiatric advice should be available to schools, courts and institutions for feeble-minded and delinquent children, and that these afford excellent opportunities for laboratory study of their conduct. Complete physical, neurological, psychiatric and psychological examination might profitably be given those persons presenting special problems to social agencies, and such examination should be available especially for delinquents. We are especially indebted to Dr. Clinton P. McCord, of Albany, N. Y., for much of the information in this important subdivision of Chapter IX.

JOHN G. SHORTALL
*President, The American Humane Association, 1884
to 1885 and 1893 to 1899*

CHAPTER X

SHORT SKETCH OF THE HISTORY OF THE AMERICAN HUMANE ASSOCIATION

THE American Humane Association was founded as the need for a national humane organization came to be felt. It is described in its annual reports as " a federation of societies and individuals for the prevention of cruelty, especially cruelty to children and animals." How well this association has fulfilled its functions can easily be understood by considering its history. Originally its founders were especially concerned in abuses connected with stock transportation. Gradually, other subjects engaged its attention until at the present time it is vitally interested in all the major humane reforms which have developed in the United States. It is also deeply concerned in extending humane propaganda and the introduction of humane education into all schools. It assists, through its agents, in forming new anticruelty societies and in reviving weak or dormant ones. Its correspondence has increased enormously; letters come from all parts of the world, asking advice.

It publishes *The National Humane Review,* which is the official organ of the anticruelty movement in this country, and prints a large amount of leaflet literature and humane tracts, which are widely distributed. Other great progressive reforms are contemplated.

This Association came into existence in 1877 as the result of a meeting of humanitarians called in Cleveland by Mr. John G. Shortall, then President of the Illinois Humane Society, to consider means for combating abuses connected with cattle transportation. Mr. Shortall's call read:

> Office of the Illinois Humane Society,
> Chicago, Sept. 15, 1877.

Dear Sir:

In pursuance of a resolution adopted by the Illinois Humane Society, looking to the calling of a convention or conference of the leading humane societies of the country, for the purpose of considering the question of the maltreatment of animals in transit between the East and West, it has been proposed that such a convention be held in the city of Cleveland, Ohio, at a place hereafter to be notified to you, on Tuesday, the ninth day of October next, at 10 A. M.

We cordially invite your presence there, feeling sure of your appreciation of the necessity of some concert of action in this important matter, important, as it is, to both producers and consumers, as well as to the cattle that are compelled to suffer the barbarous treatment that is often so wantonly inflicted upon them.

If you should be prevented from attending, please have your society appoint a proper committee to speak for it.

It is proposed that legislative action be demanded on the decision of this conference.

Very respectfully yours,

JOHN G. SHORTALL,

President, Illinois Humane Society.

Twenty-two delegates, from ten states, representing twelve societies, gathered at this now historic meeting and decided that much good would be accomplished by a permanent organization. Mr. Edwin Lee Brown, who was the first President of the Illinois Humane Society and an able and conscientious gentleman, was selected as its first President. Mr. Abraham Firth, Secretary of the Massachusetts Society for the Prevention of Cruelty to Animals, was elected Secretary. Much credit for the early work is due to the latter, who gave it much time and large financial assistance. Mrs. Caroline E. White, President of the Women's Pennsylvania Society for the Prevention of Cruelty to Animals, was present at this meeting and was placed on the Executive Committee with George T. Angell and others. The name " International Humane Society " was adopted, but this was changed at the second meeting, held in Baltimore, to the one by which it is now known, The American Humane Association. At the Baltimore meeting, Mr. Bergh and Mr. Angell were present and took part in the proceedings. A legislative agent was employed to remain at Washington to work in behalf of the passage of the cattle transportation act, then before Congress.

During the third year of the Association's existence, Mr. Zadok Street, of Salem, Ohio, traveled 18,000 miles in behalf of the Association's survey of stock transportation abuses. The frightful condition of the cattle cars caused the Association to raise a special fund of $5,000, in 1880, as prizes for the best improved cattle car. No awards were ever made, because the contestants refused to convey the rights in their inventions to the Association. The outcome of the contest, in which 710 designs were submitted, resulted in immediate improvements in the types of new cars built by the railroads. Eight gold medals were subsequently awarded the best designs. For four years the Association employed travelling agents for all, or part time, in securing additional evidence of the unfortunate lot of cattle transported by train. Stockyard agents were employed and stationed for a period at Albany and Buffalo. In 1882, a test case was brought to the courts against the Boston and Albany railroad and a conviction was obtained of the railroad officials for violations of the 28 hour law. This was a notable case and of great value to the whole cause.

The fund that had been raised for the cattle car contest was used in 1884 for paid advertisements in newspapers of every political party; also

EDWIN LEE BROWN
*First President, The American Humane
Association, 1877 to 1884 and
1889 to 1891*

in the leading religious magazines, besides those
known as agricultural, railroad, stock, etc. This
was the first nation-wide advertising campaign
ever attempted by humane organizations.

Among the generous early financial backers
of the Association were Miss Anne Wigglesworth
and Mrs. William Appleton. The latter will be
recalled as the active helper of George T. Angell
in organizing the Massachusetts Society for the
Prevention of Cruelty to Animals.

The terrible conditions governing transportation of food animals from farms and ranches to
the stockyards were vividly shown in reports
presented from time to time to the Association.
At the inaugural meeting in Cleveland, in 1877,
George A. Martin, whose professional duties had
made it necessary for him to attend the East
Buffalo stockyards daily, reported: "The live
stock traffic of the country is a long line of suffering from the West to the East. And when the
jaded, frantic, feverish animals arrive at their
eastern destination, they are hurried to the sham-
bles, their flesh little, if any better fit for human
food than so much carrion. And then the diseased and bruised animals, which are unfit from
the moment of shipment—cattle with putrid,
malignant ulcers on the lower jaw; sheep crippled with foot-rot (80,000 foot-rotten sheep
passed through East Buffalo in a single year);
ewes hurried to the cars, leaving lambs a few ·

hours old to bleat their brief lives out in the deserted pens; hogs purple with the so-called hog cholera—all these were daily sights in the great cattle yards. * * * Millions of suffering brutes which cannot speak for themselves, and thousands of consumers of diseased flesh, unconscious of the wrongs inflicted upon them, are in reality represented at your Conference in Cleveland."

The little band of humane enthusiasts was not viewed with favor by legislators, and every conceivable slander was hurled by the interests to hold up the approaching reforms. One of the commonest replies to requests for a stringent transportation law was that the reform was sought "in the interests of patent cars"—to create a market, and financial gain for the inventors who saw the need of humane transportation and were trying to solve the problem. The Association, however, sought to deal with the evils not only by legislation, but also by conciliatory negotiation with the livestock interests. Some progress was made, although it was very slight.

The reports of Zadok Street, traveling humane agent, were a long recital of infamous conditions. It almost appeared as though the vast bulk of those engaged in the livestock business were actuated by the spirit of demons. Hundreds of dead animals were taken from the railroad cars. Cripples were dragged out, by the head, ears, tail—anyhow—and left to die. In one instance a steer had been so burned to make him get up that the carcass was unfit for marketing. Other tortures were of a kind that could not be set forth in print. At places where cattle trains stopped the men who accompanied the animals walked alongside and jabbed and prodded all that were down, until they arose to their feet—if they were able to do so. Still the reformers worked in spite of the jeers of cattlemen, who referred to them as "long-haired comeouters" and in various other terms of opprobrium.

The first really great step in advance was made when the Federal Government placed the enforcement of the 28 hour law in the hands of the Department of Agriculture, and the Bureau of Animal Industry was given the task of enforcing the law. This has been done honestly and efficiently, and is being so enforced to-day. If The American Humane Association had taken up no other question than that of stock transportation it was worth while. To-day the prod is almost eliminated, and representatives of the cattleraisers, railroads, packing houses and other interests meet in conference, including representatives of The American Humane Association, to discuss plans and methods by which losses and injuries can be still further reduced. The world is learning that humanity pays.

Next to transportation, importance has attached to the starvation of cattle on the ranges and to the subject of slaughterhouse reform. Both of these were discussed at many of the annual conventions. It was shown that the losses of cattle and sheep on the great ranges, due to starvation and exposure, amounted to millions upon millions of dollars. Local anticruelty societies were powerless to accomplish much relief. In one state the law specifically exempted from punishment men who starved their stock to death. The cattle were simply turned loose to gamble with death. They had to face starvation and thirst in the awful blizzards of the western ranges. They died by tens of thousands.

The public lands were overrun with stock. No rent was paid. The range which formerly supported millions of buffalo was depleted. Men who owned cattle fought men who owned sheep for priority of grazing rights. Cattlemen, at times, were said to have killed off all the sheep they could. In two reported instances it was said that flocks of sheep were driven over precipices and dashed to pieces on the rocks below. Local societies were unable to cope with the problem; it was too vast. The American Humane Association has fought the evil with unceasing publicity, advocating that the public domain should be controlled and regulated by the Department of Agriculture in the same man-

ner that the lands included in the Forest Re-
serves are controlled, grazing privileges being
granted only to stockmen who have enough ranch
property to take care of their stock in winter.

Some improvement has been made, but the
problem still presses for solution. Education
through the agricultural colleges, the public
schools, stock markets and other avenues has
done something. There is an awakening conscience. One important factor has been the increased value of livestock, during the period
beginning with the world war. Many stockmen
who formerly gave no kind of winter care now
gather quantities of rough forage in the fall
and are able to take care of their animals in
winter. They find that it pays. There is, apparently, no single remedy for the condition and
only a gradual improvement can be looked for.
Government regulation of grazing on public
lands will help most. The herds are lessening in
size so there is less suffering. The homesteaders
are taking up more land and caring for their
stock. All this accomplishes much.

Many efforts have been made to abolish the
horrors of the slaughterhouses. One of the most
important moves in this direction was the offer
of a prize of $10,000 by the American Society
for the Prevention of Cruelty to Animals, for a
successful device, or instrument, by means of
which animals about to be slaughtered may be

promptly and effectively stunned. A special committee on slaughterhouse reform was appointed by The American Humane Association, of which Dr. F. H. Rowley, of Boston, was made chairman. The campaign against slaughterhouse cruelties has been pushed with the greatest vigor.

As The American Humane Association grew its vision developed. It used its influence from time to time to prevent the introduction of bullfighting into the United States. It fought the rodeo, round-up, wild west show, and every other form of brutal sport. It gave full support to local societies in conflicts with evils they were not powerful enough to fight single-handed. The Association was among the first to protest against the extermination of the buffalo, of wild life generally, and especially of birds.

The Association took note of evil conditions in all parts of the world, notably in South America, where (in Peru) it was reported that animals were flayed alive because of the belief that the skins so taken were more durable and flexible. Gander pulling in California was a " sport " which was checked. A live gander was suspended, its neck smeared with grease, and men on horses rode swiftly underneath, grabbing the gander by the neck, and in some instances tearing off the head. Largely due to the Association's influence transportation

conditions on cattle ships were vastly improved
and the horrors of the journey of livestock from
the United States abroad have been minimized.
The introduction of cold storage transportation
of dead meat abroad has eliminated much of the
cause for complaint, but stock transportation
in the United States is still unsatisfactory. Committees at different times reported on the need
for the humane destruction of small animals, on
the bad management of city pounds and other
abuses.   Local societies in this manner were
benefited by the latest and best available knowledge on various subjects.

In the early days of The American Humane
Association its activities were devoted exclusively to the welfare of animals.   Some of the
constituent societies, however, were engaged in
the dual work of protecting children as well as
animals, and the report of the St. Louis meeting,
in 1885, was the first to be illustrated with the
Association's new double seal, which depicted on
one side the protection of animals and on the
other the protection of children.   Delegates from
child protection societies did not attend, as such,
until the Rochester meeting in 1887.   So far as
child protection was concerned the Association
centered its efforts towards guaranteeing such
protection from every form of abuse and cruelty,
and the enforcement of laws for their protection.
Shocking abuses were discovered.   At Rochester

the convention discussed methods for dealing with fathers who deserted their families. Subsequently the treatment of children in institutions was investigated, and at Louisville, in 1889, Mr. Brown, of Chicago, declared that most fiendish cruelties had been found to have been inflicted upon children in the institutions of that city.

The horrors of child life, even so recently as 1891, were exposed at the Denver meeting, where it was reported, in the campaign against infanticide, that bodies of 3,000 children a year were consigned, even when alive, to the sewers or thrown into the river at Philadelphia. In another city, to obtain insurance money, one woman murdered her two children and her husband, for which the death penalty was inflicted. Reports of children killed on so-called baby farms were numerous. Gradually the work for children developed along broad lines, but with the central motive that the movement was not one of charity, almsgiving or welfare, but essentially one of justice and legal protection in the widest and best sense. This attitude was clearly defined on several occasions by Mr. Elbridge T. Gerry and other leaders. It was feared that, if the societies were engaged in child welfare only and the basic principle of protection was lost sight of, or at least made subservient to other features, the legal work of child protection, for which the children's societies were especially created, would be neglected or cease.

In the early days of the Association there were members sufficiently far-sighted to realize that it should have a charter of incorporation, and at the Baltimore meeting, in 1878, it was decided to ask Congress for such a charter, to include " all the legal powers that such a society ought to have in carrying on a national humane work." This resolution was reaffirmed a year later, at Chicago, but it was not acted upon. However, the subject cropped up at several conventions, but there were differences of opinion as to what should be the main purposes of the Association and how far its jurisdiction should extend. At the Cincinnati Convention of 1886, President Gordon declared " The scope of the Association is the extended scope of the societies which compose it. * * * Its mission is to remedy universal cruelties by universal remedies, to foster a national recognition of the duties we owe those who are helpless, to spread knowledge on humane organizations where such do not exist."

Several times the question of disbanding the Association was discussed, notably at the Pittsburgh Convention of 1884. Even some whose names rank high in the history of the movement favored this course, but the Association held on. Its income, however, was far from being assured, and officers, agents and organizers were appointed intermittently and only for short periods, the expense being borne usually by a few persons specially interested. At the Buffalo meeting, in 1901, Dr. William O. Stillman, then on the Executive Committee, in a paper on " The Problems of Humane Extension," came out strongly for a development of the Association and astounded some of his hearers by advocating that there should be an endowment of not less than half a million dollars with which to put a national work on an adequate footing. A year later, at Albany, a special committee on organization again recommended that the Association be nationally incorporated as " the natural development of any philanthropic movement where effective work is needed." There was considerable opposition to the proposal, some prominent humanitarians fearing that it would involve the setting up of a big national machine, and that money would flow to a national treasury which ought to be devoted to local purposes. Dr. Stillman, Mrs. Caroline Earle White and Mr. James M. Brown were amongst those who favored incorporation. By agreement consideration was deferred to the Cincinnati meeting, in 1903, when incorporation was definitely agreed upon.

Subsequent events have proved that the fears of those who opposed incorporation were ground-

less. While an effective national organization
has been built up, local humane societies have
benefited rather than suffered, financially and in
other ways. Many societies have been preserved
from extinction, others have been reorganized
and saved. In times of crisis local societies have
had the help of the national body in their struggles. The Association has brought about cohe-
sion, it has inspired local societies to greater effort, lifted them from the depths of hopeless
despair and pointed the way to a successful
future. Many societies which have become prosperous have freely admitted that much of their
success is the direct result of the guidance and
encouragement received from national headquarters, and from its traveling agents and
organizers.

An important part of the missionary work of
The American Humane Association has been
shown by its publication of a large amount of
leaflet literature. Tons upon tons of these leaflets have been widely distributed either by sale at
cost or free of charge. The demand for these
humane tracts has been marvelously large. They
have served to create humane sentiment; also to
furnish necessary advice where people desired to
start new anticruelty societies or where reforms
were demanded. A leaflet entitled " First Aid to
Small Animals " has supplemented the one
printed on "First Aid for Horses," which was

distributed on request and without charge to the extent of 150,000 copies.

Many very valuable leaflets on " Humane Education " have been printed and widely distributed. The Association has very actively pushed the work of introducing instruction in humane education, hoping to gain entrance into all public schools in the United States. Twenty-three states already have laws requiring such teaching. In this connection the Association is now planning for the creation of a training school, or college, where humane agents may receive special instruction to fit them, not only for office or field work, for local societies, and for the proper care and management of cases of abuse of little children and animals, but especially to act as lecturers to give instruction in teachers' training schools and institutes, and before public bodies wherever humane instruction is required. The American Humane Association, through the efforts of President Stillman, founded *The National Humane Review,* which is greatly assisting the humane educational work being carried on all over the United States and in foreign countries. The foreign missionary work of the Association has assumed large proportions and promises even greater development in the future. The magazine is proving remarkably acceptable and successful.

It is a matter of special interest that " Hu-

mane Sunday " and " Be Kind to Animals
Week " were introduced into the United States
through the initiative and efforts of The American Humane Association, which has done much
to make these occasions the great yearly celebration of the humane world in this country. The
yearly delivery of Mercy Sunday sermons by
clergymen in England had been in vogue for
some time before it was taken up on this side of
the Atlantic. It remained for Americans to develop the idea of a week being set aside for
special secular observances in behalf of mercy
and kindness. During this week visits are made
to shelters for children and animals, proclama-
tions are issued by many governors and mayors,
pet animal shows are held and work horse
parades are conducted. There are exhibits of
humane posters and of bird houses; humane literature is distributed and special humane relief
work done. Addresses, personally and by radio,
are made before men's and women's clubs, at
schools and special gatherings. Many schools
have appropriate exercises, which are assisted by
Boy and Girl Scouts; medals are given, humane
motion picture films are shown and the newspapers print humane stories. Humane publicity
is the keynote of the observance and banners and
placards are plentifully exhibited in stores, on
houses and wagons, and on animals. People

wear humane buttons, and sometimes animals are similarly decorated.

Humane Sunday has been very largely observed by the churches, especially since several denominations have publicly declared in favor of humane education. Thousands of pulpits proclaim the duty of humanity. The text " Blessed are the Merciful " is frequently chosen as a theme for discourses. Tens of thousands of humane posters are made by school children for prizes, for in this way they become greatly interested in humane education and anticruelty problems. More is being done in these ways for humane advancement than the world realizes and the next generation of Americans will show the result by a higher and nobler grade of citizenship. These observances may well be imitated in every country.

One of the most important reforms which the Association has undertaken has been the prevention of cruel trapping. It has been found that millions of small animals, and sometimes birds and domestic animals in great numbers, have been seized by steel traps and left to die terrible deaths. Traps are often not visited by the trapper for days. The animals held in traps are apt to die from starvation, or cold, often suffering lingering agony. Some are eaten alive by their natural enemies. Muskrats have had their eyes picked out by crows. The number of animals involved is estimated by Dr. Hornaday to amount to thirty millions yearly. Public sentiment is beginning to awaken. Reform will come. Fur farms save much lingering suffering. Humane traps, which kill animals instantly, are gaining public favor.

During recent years the work of The American Humane Association has steadily extended. This is the end which has been constantly sought and the best proof of its success. Calls for its aid have come from all parts of the United States. The response has been limited only by the funds at its disposal which enables it to employ agents, and while the income has increased the calls upon the Association have increased in still greater proportion. An endowment has been created, although it is far from the goal set by Dr. Stillman in his address at the Buffalo meeting and the actual needs of the Association. Without question it is inadequate for the needs of the work and should be greatly increased so as to safeguard the future of national humane operations.

Among the numerous investigations into cruelties of unusual proportions may be mentioned the oilfields investigations of 1922 and 1923. In this instance the investigation referred particularly to the Arkansas oilfields, although it was also shown that great cruelties had been practised in other fields. In the greed to open up new sources of oil heavy machinery was hauled by mule teams through fields until they were converted into bogs and morasses. To force the animals to do the almost impossible, mules were whipped, beaten and pounded until they dropped. The Arkansas highways in many places were little better than the bogs that were encountered on the sidetracks to the wells, and reports were received of mules being drowned in the deep mud-holes while straining at their loads. Publication of the facts in newspapers throughout the United States brought about an improvement in the situation, but even at the best, conditions were bad, due to the fact that most people in the oil regions apparently thought only of financial gain and the public authorities took no real steps to end the abuses.

Among the services which have been rendered to local humane work, the sending of experts from headquarters, in times of need, has resulted advantageously. In many sections local difficulties have been relieved. Societies have been aided in campaigns to secure funds; others have sought guidance in the preparation of plans for the general development of their work. As a result the movement has made great advances in many sections, for the work has been extended and shelters and other buildings have been erected. Hundreds of lectures also have been given by representatives from headquarters, frequently resulting in a more favorable attitude on the part of the public. Many cities have been induced to turn over to anticruelty societies for animals the public pounds, together with the work of collecting and disposing of stray, homeless and unlicensed dogs, thus doing away with the horrors of many ill-managed city pounds.

One of the important undertakings of The American Humane Association has been its introduction into the United States of international humane conferences. The first one to be held was that which met at Washington, D. C., under the honorary presidency of Wm. H. Taft, President of the United States. This was held on October 10-15, 1910, and was very largely attended by humanitarians from all parts of the United States and by representatives from more than thirty foreign countries. The deliberations of this great gathering resulted in many practical reforms. There was an extensive display of humane literature, posters and objects of special interest, filling several large rooms. The sessions of the conference served to bring humanitarians together from many countries and to unify humane methods and practices. The meeting excited much commendation and praise.

On October 22 to 27, 1923, another International Conference was held in New York City. This was largely attended by delegates from at home and abroad. Hundreds of Americans took part in its proceedings, which were marked by harmony and enthusiasm. Special emphasis was laid on reforms in slaughterhouse methods and transportation abuses, as well as trapping cruelties and blood sports. Child protection received much attention, as many vital topics were discussed, including child protection in its broader aspects, special policies pursued, and agencies instrumental in child helping. The value of recreational facilities and posters in child saving was presented. Child protection service in England, France, India and Japan was ably discussed; also motion picture regulation and the problems of delinquency and children's code commissions. The need for children's shelters and paid agents was strongly brought out. The great value of International Conferences was emphasized and undoubtedly others will follow.

A word in reference to some of the earlier Presidents. Mr. John G. Shortall in 1884 was elected to succeed Mr. Edwin Lee Brown, who had held office continuously since 1877, when the work was first started. He put new life in the movement, but resigned at the end of his term in favor of Rev. G. E. Gordon, of Milwaukee, who was elected to office during three years, from 1885 to 1887. At a meeting held in Toronto in 1888, Hon. Elbridge T. Gerry, the father of the child protection movement, was elected President. At the end of his term, that sincere humanitarian, Edwin Lee Brown, of Chicago, was again elected President by the elections for 1889 and 1890. He died in 1891, after nearly two years in office. Mr. L. H. Eaton, of Pittsburgh, was then elected for the years 1891 and 1892. Mr. Shortall was again elected President in 1892 and served until 1898. During his Presidency he presided over an International Humane Congress, held in Chicago in 1893.

At the Columbus meeting in 1899, Mr. J. M. Brown, of Toledo, Ohio, was elected President and served until succeeded by President Stillman, in 1905, except for a period at the close of President Brown's term, when Dr. Albert Leffingwell served part of a term. Mr. Brown was President of the Toledo Humane Society until his death in 1909. It was during his administration that the Association was incorporated, under the laws of the District of Columbia, in 1903.

It would require a volume to recite in detail the work of the men and women who have contributed to the success of the Association. Among those who have served as honorary vice-presidents may be mentioned several Presidents of the United States, notably Hon. Grover Cleveland, Hon. Warren G. Harding and Hon. Calvin Coolidge, while former President Wm. H. Taft has been listed among such officers for about eighteen years and has always shown marked personal interest. Of prominent ecclesiastics, there may be mentioned the names of Cardinals Gibbons and Dougherty; Rt. Rev. James F. Sweeny, D.D.; Rev. Charles Scanlon, LL.D.; Rev. S. Z. Batten, D.D., and others who have been honorary vice-presidents. Many splendid women are also included in this list, such as that genuine humanitarian Minnie Maddern Fiske; Mrs. George T. Angell, the devoted wife of the great humane pioneer, and Mrs. Jack London, whose husband's labors caused the starting of the Jack London Clubs and reforms in behalf of performing animals. Senator Peter G. Gerry, the oldest son of the illustrious founder and builder of child protection work, has long been closely associated with The American Humane Association, as its first Vice-President and one of its most valued directors. Senator Gerry's labors for the humane cause have been of great value and stamp him as a worthy son of a noble sire.